SIMPLE SUPERFOOD SOUPS

SIMPLE SUPERFOOD SOUPS

75 Nourishing Recipes for a Healthier You

PAMELA ELLGEN

Photography by Darren Muir

ROCKRIDGE
PRESS

For general information on our other products and services or to obtain technical support, please contact our Customer Care Department within the United States at (866) 744-2665, or outside the United States at (510) 253-0500.

Rockridge Press publishes its books in a variety of electronic and print formats. Some content that appears in print may not be available in electronic books, and vice versa.

TRADEMARKS: Rockridge Press and the Rockridge Press logo are trademarks or registered trademarks of Callisto Media Inc. and/or its affiliates, in the United States and other countries, and may not be used without written permission. All other trademarks are the property of their respective owners. Rockridge Press is not associated with any product or vendor mentioned in this book.

Interior and Cover Designer: Amanda Kirk
Art Producer: Janice Ackerman
Editor: Kayla Park
Production Editor: Jenna Dutton

Photography: © 2020 Darren Muir
Food styling by Yolanda Muir

ISBN: Print   978-1-64611-470-2
          eBook 978-1-64611-471-9

R0

FOR RICH

CONTENTS

INTRODUCTION

All over the globe, soups bring people together around a welcoming pot—whether it's rich *tonjiru* cooked in a *donabe* in Japan or fragrant lamb stew cooked in a *tagine* in Morocco. Soups unite different cultures and disparate ingredients in one pot.

Some of the best soups I have ever tasted have distinct origins, developed and refined over years of tradition. And yet, soups invite creativity and a blurring of cultural lines and even the rules of cooking. Consider how the French classic *moules marinières*—steamed mussels in white wine, shallots, and cream—becomes something new entirely with fragrant Indian saffron, coconut milk, and rice noodles. Or, imagine a classic parsnip bisque transformed from the heavy cream–laden soup to a healthy, vegan version topped with a California-inspired pomegranate pesto.

A soup like this is not the work of one man. It is the result of a constantly refined tradition. There are nearly a thousand years of history in this soup.
—WILLA CATHER

Whatever you have in your pantry or refrigerator has a place in your soup pot—though perhaps not all at once. Vegetables from the farmers' market, fresh herbs from your garden, a handful of extra wheat berries, and that can of tomatoes languishing on the shelf all belong in the pot. Soups are the ultimate luxury of being frugal.

One of my earliest food memories is of my mom's beef stew. She would put everything in the slow cooker in the morning and let it simmer all day, filling the house with promises of a good meal. Those aromas comforted us when we stumbled in the door, exhausted after a long day of hiking in the chilly Pacific Northwest.

To feel safe and warm on a cold wet night, all you really need is soup.
—LAURIE COLWIN

Soups are also flexible and adaptable to whatever your dietary preferences happen to be. When I first moved to Santa Barbara, we attended a church that hosted weekly dinners in the spring and fall. I soon realized that the meals left the vegans among us hungry—one cannot live on side dishes and salads alone. I quickly took on the job of official soup-maker. Each soup had to be good. It had to be unique. And, it had to serve 100 people. While I was at it, I made my soups gluten-free. The soups performed brilliantly, and even the omnivores begged for the recipes, especially the hearty Fire-Roasted Vegan Chili (page 128) and soothing Vegetable Pho (page 115).

Given soup's versatility and its willingness to embrace all kinds of foods, it's also the perfect place to sneak in, or even load up on, superfoods.

WHY SUPERFOODS?

'm going to let you in on a little secret. It's one that few in the health-food or food-marketing industries want you to know. Nearly every plant-based whole food is a superfood. A superfood is simply a food that, when eaten in normal quantities, delivers documented health benefits. You could have a kitchen filled with superfoods and not even know it.

For example, a study published in the *International Journal of Food Sciences Nutrition* had subjects eat roughly two cups of broccoli per day. After only 10 days of adding the cruciferous vegetable to their diets, the participants' C-reactive protein, a marker of inflammation, decreased by 48 percent. That's pretty impressive for one of the most common and inexpensive vegetables found at the grocery store. You can find references to all studies cited in the back of the book (see pages 146–151).

You don't have to search high and low for obscure ingredients grown in the far reaches of the Earth, on the highest mountaintop, by the oldest living group of people. Sure, it makes for clever marketing, but you can find high concentrations of antioxidants, phytochemicals, vitamins, and minerals in foods you already know. They may be growing right in your backyard garden or readily available at your local farmers' market or grocery store.

Here's where they're *not* found: in processed, packaged foods, such as goji berry cereal, maca chocolate truffles, cranberry pomegranate granola bars, or broccoli puffs. If it comes in a powder and has a shelf life measured in years, it's probably not worth the money. Think about it this way—if it comes from a plant, it's probably a superfood. If it was *made* in a plant, it's probably not.

Michael Pollan argues this point in his book *In Defense of Food*. He says, for health and longevity, to eat food, but not too much, and mostly plants. In addition to Pollan, I also draw from the research of Dr. Michael Greger in his book *How Not to Diet*. He thoroughly explores all the major conditions afflicting humans today and shows which foods we can eat to prevent or even reverse them—many of those foods comprise my top 15 superfoods list.

I debated whether to use any meat at all in this book. But I concluded that the longest-lived people on earth—those who live in the "blue zone" regions—consume *mostly* but not *entirely* plants. (Except for the American blue zone in Loma Linda, California, where people choose a vegan diet for religious reasons.) And, in each place, local cuisines may include, for example, a roasted chicken, or goat cheese, or fresh fish. The epidemiological evidence suggests there is room in a healthy diet for moderation. That looks different for each person. Hence, many recipes in this book are entirely plant-based—but not all.

Finally, a quick word on organics. Food grown without herbicides, pesticides, and chemical fertilizers is ideal. Not only is it free from (or mostly free from) chemical residues, it also has more nutrients than non-organic foods. However, don't let perfect be the enemy of the good. Choose what's fresh, what's available, and what you can afford.

The Best Superfoods for Soups

Superfoods and soups are meant for each other. Sure, salads are a great way to dish up colorful superfoods, but sometimes you want something warm and comforting. And, soups make it easy to get a lot of nutrition without a massive plate of greens in front of you.

The trick to getting the most nutritional bang for your buck in soup-making is choosing foods that become more nutritious when cooked or are more enjoyable, so you'll eat more of them. Also, some of the best soups are topped with a generous garnish for added texture and nutrition. This is a great place for things like broccoli sprouts, nutritional yeast, hemp seeds, pomegranate seeds, and other superfoods that offer big benefits in small portions.

All the superfoods and groups of foods listed here are expounded on in many of the recipes.

1. **Cruciferous vegetables:** Broccoli, kale, cabbage, and watercress are all standouts in the cruciferous vegetable category. They are potent cancer fighters, protect DNA from mutation, improve immunity, and lower cholesterol, to name just a few of their superfood powers. Other tasty options include bok choy, gai lan (Chinese broccoli), and rapini.

2. **Legumes:** Lentils, chickpeas, black beans, white beans, and kidney beans all bring a host of nutrients to your soups. Fiber protects against stroke, diabetes, heart disease, and colon cancer. It also improves the health of your gut microbiome for a better mood and better digestion. The phytates in legumes and other seeds help detoxify excess iron, kill cancer cells, and improve bone density. Moreover, replacing meat with plant sources of protein can reduce your risk for all vascular diseases and cancers.

3. **Dark leafy greens:** Collards, spinach, arugula, and chard are my favorite dark leafy greens for adding to soup. (So is kale, but it's included in the cruciferous vegetables category.) Dark greens are loaded with antioxidants and phytonutrients that reduce inflammation and fight oxidative stress.

4. **Sweet potato:** This root vegetable is loaded with potassium, essential for reducing stroke risk and improving

muscle contractions and nerve signals. It's also filled with fiber, manganese, and vitamins A and C.

5. **Herbs:** Even a small amount of herbs, such as basil, rosemary, mint, oregano, and cilantro, has been shown to offer health benefits. For example, a teaspoon of dried oregano reduced stroke risk in one study. A half cup of roughly chopped basil—the amount you'd find in a couple tablespoons of pesto—supplies your entire daily value of vitamin K, which is important for bone health and blood clotting.

6. **Berries:** For an exceptional boost of antioxidants, look to berries and other dark-colored fruits, including blueberries, goji berries, raspberries, and strawberries.

7. **Spices:** Everyday spices such as turmeric, cinnamon, cumin, paprika, and chili all offer a generous dose of phytonutrients and antioxidants—in addition to making your food taste delicious. For example, turmeric has been shown to reduce the risk for all cancers. One study found even smelling saffron reduced anxiety and cortisol levels.

8. **Nuts and seeds:** Like beans, nuts and seeds are a good source of phytates and fiber. One study found that eating just four Brazil nuts lowered cholesterol for up to one month.

9. **Garlic and onions:** I add garlic and onions to nearly all my soups because they taste good, but their phytonutrients are also good for you. The same compounds that give you fragrant breath are also potent cancer fighters.

10. **Whole grains:** Even everyday whole grains, such as wheat and oats, are superfoods. So, too, are millet, buckwheat, and quinoa, though they are technically seeds. Whole grains are especially helpful for keeping your cardiovascular system healthy.

11. **Sea vegetables:** Sea vegetables, such as kombu and other seaweeds, are a rich source of iodine and trace minerals. They also lend a refreshing sea taste to food without using fish or shellfish.

12. **Fermented soy:** Soybeans are a good source of protein, fiber, and phytonutrients. I cook frequently with tempeh, miso, and soy sauce.

Fermented soy is easier to digest and offers probiotic benefits to nurture a healthy gut microbiome.

13. **Healthy fats:** Coconut, olives, and avocado tie for the top superfood healthy fat. The plant-based fat in these foods helps you absorb the nutrients in other superfoods. Plus, they taste really good.

14. **Other fruits:** Fruits such as apple, mango, citrus, grapes, and pomegranate all contain beneficial phytochemicals, antioxidants, vitamins, and minerals. Most are healthiest when consumed raw, so in this book, I use them as a garnish or stirred into a finished dish.

15. **Chocolate:** I'm not including chocolate just because I love it—it's an excellent source of antioxidants and healthy fats. Chocolate also adds complexity and depth to some of my favorite soups, including Chicken Mole (page 126).

Building Your Superfood Pantry

Superfoods are found not only in the produce bin but also in the pantry. Stock up on these essentials and you'll be well on your way to making many of the recipes in this book.

A traditional grocery store will offer everything you'll need to make superfood soups. However, a trip to a health-food store might save you some time and money. I find it's easier to find what I'm looking for in a short time when I'm not walking down aisles of candy and processed foods. And, health-food stores often offer healthy staples in bulk, such as dried beans, nuts, and spices.

Here are the top items to have on your shelf:

OILS

I cook with extra-virgin olive oil most frequently. When you use it in cooking as opposed to as a finishing garnish or in a salad dressing, save your money and purchase an everyday olive oil. Kirkland has an organic extra-virgin olive oil that's a good price and tastes amazing. Canola oil is another option and has a neutral flavor that makes it versatile. Coconut oil has risen to superfood status in recent decades, but it may not live up to the hype. Most of its fat is saturated, which, despite fad diets that claim otherwise, is still a significant contributor to cardiovascular disease.

HERBS

Most herbs are best when fresh—parsley, cilantro, basil, and tarragon especially. But there are a few worth stocking in your pantry because they retain their flavor when dried. These include oregano, bay leaf, marjoram, and sage.

SPICES

Spices are one of my favorite superfoods because they're inexpensive, a little goes a long way, and they keep for much longer than other ingredients. Here are the essentials: cinnamon, ginger, turmeric, curry powder (a blend of spices), smoked paprika, saffron, red pepper flakes, and whole black peppercorns.

CANNED GOODS

Canned goods may not seem like a likely source of superfoods, but they might just surprise you. Canned beans make for a quick supper and are just as healthy as the beans you cook from dry. And canned tomatoes have even more lycopene than fresh tomatoes because cooking improves lycopene's bioavailability. I keep my pantry stocked with canned black beans, kidney beans, cannellini beans, and chickpeas.

DRY GOODS

Stock your pantry with dried legumes, including black beans, kidney beans, chickpeas, and lentils. Also choose nuts, including walnuts, almonds, and cashews, and seeds, including hemp, flaxseed, and sesame seeds. These don't have an indefinite shelf life, so purchase only what you think you'll use in the next three months or sooner. Also stock your pantry with whole-grain pasta, including spaghetti, penne, and elbow or shell types and other whole grains, such as freekeh, farro, quinoa, and wild rice.

FLAVOR BOOSTERS

The most frequently used flavor booster in my kitchen is soy sauce. I use a gluten-free, low-sodium tamari. I also keep white miso, tomato paste, red chili paste, Dijon mustard, capers, olives, and preserved lemons on hand. None are essential, but they do appear a handful of times throughout this book and pack not only flavor but also essential micronutrients.

Equipment and Tools

You don't need fancy equipment to make a good soup—just a pot and a wooden spoon will do the trick. That said, there are a few other things I cook with frequently that you may want to have on hand:

» **4-QUART AND 8-QUART POTS** Both medium and large pots with lids will come in handy for soup- and broth-making.

» **CHEF'S KNIFE** A sharp chef's knife can mince and dice vegetables into just the right size.

» **DUTCH OVEN** For hearty soups and stews made in the oven, a Dutch oven is the way to go. It can start on the stovetop and transfer to the oven. A 5-quart size will accommodate soup for up to a dozen people.

» **FINE-MESH SIEVE** Use this for straining ingredients, such as aromatics, from broths.

» **IMMERSION BLENDER** For pureed soups, an immersion blender is essential. You could also use a countertop blender, but be careful! Steaming soup can literally blow the lid off your blender and bathe you and your kitchen in scalding liquid.

» **LIQUID MEASURING CUPS** Use a liquid measuring cup for broths and wine.

Getting Started

"Only the pure of heart can make a good soup," Beethoven is often quoted as saying. I'm not sure purity has anything to do with it, but good ingredients and good technique go a long way. Here are a few techniques for building a great soup:

- **Start with flavor:** Combine a mixture of finely diced onion, celery, carrot, and a pinch of salt in olive oil. Cook for about 10 minutes, stirring frequently, until soft and fragrant. This base is called *mirepoix* in French. In Italy, it's *soffritto* and may include herbs and rendered pork fat. Some version of soffritto can be found all over the world building flavor into soups, stews, and all kinds of dishes.

- **Use good broth:** The broth or stock you use should be delicious enough that it could function as a soup on its own. In the same way you shouldn't cook with a wine you wouldn't drink, don't make soup with a broth you wouldn't enjoy a few spoonfuls of on its own.

- **Take your time:** Most soups benefit from a generous amount of time to allow the flavors to come together. If you don't have the luxury of standing over the stove for an hour or more, let a slow cooker or pressure cooker do the work for you. Or, make the soup a day ahead and then cover, chill, and refrigerate it overnight. This will bring all the flavors together.

- **Add herbs late:** Tender herbs, such as parsley, basil, cilantro, and tarragon, as well as other soft leafy greens, such as watercress and spinach, offer the most nutrition and flavor when they're, essentially, uncooked and simply warmed in the soup before serving.

Just as anyone can enjoy superfoods regardless of their budget or health savviness, anyone can make soup!

STOCKS AND BROTHS

Chapter 1 features recipes for homemade stocks and broths. Each contains superfoods in its own right, such as sea vegetables in the Kombu Dashi (page 8), mushrooms in the Mushroom Broth (page 6), and copious amounts of vegetables in the Superfood Vegetable Broth (page 2). The broths are designed to be drinkable on their own—not that you would be likely to pour a cup of them, but more so that they're delicious without anything added to them. Broth forms a significant percentage of the soup, so start with the good stuff.

Nevertheless, everyone gets pressed for time. Don't feel pressure to make your broth from scratch every time. All recipes in this book call for one of the broths from chapter 1, but if you don't have time to make it from scratch, no worries! Just choose a store-bought brand that tastes good to you. The only exception to this is Kombu Dashi (page 8). It has such a subtle, mild flavor and isn't widely available as a broth in the supermarket.

STORING SOUP

Unless you serve meals to a large family every night, you'll likely have leftovers. Here are tips for storing:

1. **Chill your soup before covering it.** This reduces the likelihood of bacteria growing. Otherwise, the lid traps in the heat.

2. **Store soups and garnishes separately.** Sometimes it's tough to tell what's part of the soup and what's a garnish. When in doubt, store them separately.

3. **Store plant-based soups for up to 3 days in the refrigerator.** Soups that contain meat can be stored for up to 2 days in the refrigerator. You may be able to go longer, but I play it safe in my kitchen.

4. **Freezing soup is also an excellent way to get started on a meal for next week or next month.** To freeze, make sure the soup is thoroughly chilled first. Transfer it to a freezer-safe container, such as a freezer bag or plastic or glass container, then seal and freeze for up to 3 months. Soups containing pasta, raw soups, and soups containing raw garnishes do not freeze well.

Using the Recipes

The recipes have been organized according to the soup ingredients. Each recipe showcases at least one superfood ingredient and highlights its benefits. That means there are a lot of scientific references throughout. That might come as a surprise in a cookbook. My premise in this book is that so many everyday ingredients are superfood heroes. They might not be as sexy sounding as goji berries and maca, but that doesn't make them any less beneficial for your health. To back it up, I share the evidence, while trying to keep things light and easily digestible. (Sorry, couldn't resist!)

Each recipe comes with recipe labels. Here is an explanation of each type:

- **Dairy-Free** contains no butter, milk, cheese, or other source of dairy

- **Easy Prep** can be made with minimal steps, dishes, or hands-on work

- **Gluten-Free** contains no wheat, barley, rye, or other source of gluten

Important note: **When soy sauce or miso paste is called for, choose a gluten-free version, if needed.**

- **Vegan** contains no animal products at all, including dairy, eggs, meat, fish, or honey

- **Vegetarian** contains no meat or fish but may contain dairy or eggs

Each recipe also comes with a tip. Here is an explanation of each type:

- **Power up!** A tip for how to make the soup even more superfood filled

- **Prep tip** A tip about how to prepare or source your ingredients to make life easier for you or to explain a complicated process

- **Simplify it!** A tip about how to make preparation easier. Often these tips include slow cooker options.

- **Substitute it!** A tip about how to use another ingredient in place of one that is expensive or difficult to find, or how to make a soup vegan

- **Taste tip** A tip about how to make the food even tastier. It may involve a bit more work, such as sourcing the best ingredients.

CHAPTER ONE

Stocks and Broths

Stocks and broths can be great bases for soups, or nourishing and comforting sipped on their own. A broth usually refers to a liquid made with meat and vegetables, whereas a stock is a liquid made with bones. A broth adds flavor and nutrition. A stock adds flavor and body.

Making your own broth before making soup may seem like a frivolous extra step. Why make two recipes for one dish? Here's why—broth should be drinkable on its own. You should take a sip and think, "Oh, I would love another spoonful of that!" Can the same be said for the cartons of broth and prepared bouillon cubes in the grocery store? Usually, no—although there are some artisan brands popping up that rival a homemade version.

Another reason to make your own is it's probably going to be a lot healthier because you're starting with fresh ingredients and not adding preservatives.

This chapter includes my favorite broths and stocks. All can be used to make the soups in this book.

SUPERFOOD VEGETABLE BROTH

Dairy-Free
Easy Prep
Gluten-Free
Vegan
Makes: 4 quarts
Prep time: 10 minutes
Cook time: 40 minutes

As it turns out, all the vegetable scraps you might have tossed into your compost bin are loaded with nutrients and flavor. Put them to work in this frugal and healthy superfood broth. The recipe calls for specific ingredients, but if you're missing one or two, swap them for what you have that has a similar flavor profile. Or simply leave it out. The quantities are a rough estimate, not a hard and fast rule.

½ cup roughly chopped onion

½ cup roughly chopped carrot

½ cup roughly chopped celery

2 or 3 large garlic cloves, smashed

1 or 2 tomato cores

1 or 2 bell pepper cores

Handful mushroom stems

Handful fresh herb stems, such as thyme and parsley

4 quarts water

1 bunch kale stems, roughly chopped

1 broccoli stem, roughly chopped

1 to 2 teaspoons sea salt

1. In a large pot over high heat, combine the onion, carrot, celery, garlic, tomato, bell pepper, mushroom stems, herb stems, and water. Bring to a simmer. Reduce the heat to medium-low to keep the water at a gentle simmer for 20 minutes.

2. Add the kale and broccoli stems and cook for 15 minutes more.

3. Season with salt until the broth tastes good to you.

4. Strain the broth through a fine-mesh sieve set over a bowl. Discard or compost the vegetables.

5. Use the broth or chill and refrigerate in a covered container for up to 3 days, or freeze for up to 3 months.

PREP TIP Save vegetable scraps and place them in the freezer until you are ready to make the broth. The quantities don't have to be exact, so just use what you have.

Per Serving (1 cup): Total calories: 10; Total fat: 0g; Saturated fat: 0g; Carbohydrates: 2g; Sodium: 156mg; Fiber: 1g; Protein: 1g

ROASTED VEGETABLE BROTH

Dairy-Free
Gluten-Free
Vegan
Makes: 4 quarts
Prep time:
10 minutes
Cook time:
1 hour, 10 minutes

Roasting vegetables brings out even more flavor, as the sugars in the vegetables caramelize in the oven. This broth rivals chicken broth in its depth of flavor and can be used interchangeably. No, it doesn't taste like chicken, but it does taste really good. The mushrooms add valuable phytonutrients as well as umami, or "savory taste."

2 onions, quartered

2 carrots, scrubbed and cut into 2-inch chunks

2 celery stalks, cut into 2-inch chunks

1 cup cremini mushrooms

2 tablespoons extra-virgin olive oil

Sea salt

4 garlic cloves, smashed

¼ cup dry white wine

4 flat-leaf parsley sprigs

2 thyme sprigs

1 rosemary sprig

1 teaspoon peppercorns

4 quarts water

1. Preheat the oven to 400°F.

2. Spread the onions, carrots, celery, and mushrooms on a rimmed sheet pan. Drizzle the olive oil over the vegetables and gently toss to coat. Season with salt.

3. Roast the vegetables for 20 to 25 minutes, or until gently browned. Transfer the vegetables to a large pot set over medium-high heat.

4. Add the garlic and cook for about 30 seconds, or just until fragrant. Add the white wine and cook for 2 to 3 minutes until reduced by about half.

5. Add the parsley, thyme, rosemary, peppercorns, and water and bring the broth to a simmer. Reduce the heat to medium-low and simmer for 30 to 40 minutes, until the broth tastes rich and delicious.

Strain the broth through a fine-mesh sieve set over a bowl. Discard or compost the vegetables.

6. Use the broth or chill and refrigerate in a covered container for up to 3 days, or freeze for up to 3 months.

TASTE TIP If you eat dairy products, consider adding a Parmesan rind to this broth for even more flavor and body. Add it in step 5 along with the herbs and peppercorns.

Per Serving (1 cup): Total calories: 30; Total fat: 2g; Saturated fat: 0g; Carbohydrates: 3g; Sodium: 11mg; Fiber: 1g; Protein: 1g

MUSHROOM BROTH

Dairy-Free
Gluten-Free
Vegan
Makes:
4 quarts
Prep time:
10 minutes
Cook time:
50 minutes

Mushrooms take center stage in this flavorful broth. Even white mushrooms—often called "plain mushrooms"—offer significant nutritional benefits.

1 tablespoon extra-virgin olive oil

1 small carrot, diced

1 small leek, cleaned well and diced

2 garlic cloves, smashed

1 pound white mushrooms

2 ounces dried wild mushrooms

1 bay leaf

2 thyme sprigs

2 parsley sprigs

1 teaspoon peppercorns

4 quarts water

1. In a large pot over medium-high heat, heat the olive oil. Add the carrot and leek. Sauté for about 5 minutes until the vegetables begin to brown, increasing the heat if needed.

2. Add the garlic, mushrooms, bay leaf, thyme, parsley, peppercorns, and water. Bring the broth to a simmer, then reduce the heat and cook, uncovered, for about 45 minutes.

3. Strain the broth through a fine-mesh sieve set over a bowl. Discard or compost the vegetables. If any sediment remains from the dried mushrooms, line the sieve with a paper coffee filter and strain the broth again.

4. Use the broth or chill and refrigerate in a covered container for up to 3 days, or freeze for up to 3 months.

SIMPLIFY IT! If this seems like a lot of effort for a simple mushroom broth, omit the sautéing in step 1. You can also use herb and vegetable scraps, as described in the Superfood Vegetable Broth (page 2). The important thing here is the tremendous volume of mushrooms.

Per Serving (1 cup): Total calories: 22; Total fat: 1g; Saturated fat: 0g; Carbohydrates: 3g; Sodium: 5mg; Fiber: 1g; Protein: 1g

KOMBU DASHI

Dairy-Free
Easy Prep
Gluten-Free
Vegan
Makes:
2 quarts
Prep time:
35 minutes
Cook time:
45 minutes

This broth offers a tasty and easy way to venture into the uncharted waters of sea vegetables—a group of superfoods with the potential to ward off breast cancer and metabolic syndrome. They're one of the more exotic, or even intimidating, superfoods in this book. For a long time, I wasn't even sure where to source them. The beach? Look for dried sea vegetables, such as kombu, dulce, and wakame, in the supplements section of the health-food store, or online. While they do have superfood potential, skip the capsules of sea vegetable powder, or making them a staple food. More than 15 grams of sea vegetables every day can suppress thyroid function.

2 pieces kombu   **2 quarts water**
   (about ½ ounce)

1. In a large pot, combine the kombu and water. Let sit for 30 minutes for the kombu to reconstitute.

2. Set the pot over medium-low heat and slowly bring the water to the barest simmer. Immediately, remove the kombu and remove the pot from the heat.

3. Use the broth or chill and refrigerate in a covered container for up to 3 days, or freeze for up to 3 months.

POWER UP! Add a handful of dried shiitake mushrooms to the pot in step 1 to add umami mushroom flavor and nutrients to the broth.

Per Serving (1 cup): Total calories: 4; Total fat: 0g; Saturated fat: 0g; Carbohydrates: 1g; Sodium: 78mg; Fiber: 1g; Protein: 0g

MISO BROTH

Makes:
2 quarts

Prep time:
10 minutes

Cook time:
35 minutes

This flavorful broth is drinkable on its own or makes a perfect base for other soups. To preserve its probiotics, stir in the miso after removing the soup from the heat.

1 ounce shiitake
   mushrooms

6 garlic
   cloves, smashed

2 pieces kombu
   (about ½ ounce)

1 yellow
   onion, quartered

1 celery stalk, cut
   into 2-inch pieces

1 carrot, cut into
   2-inch pieces

2 quarts water

¼ cup white
   miso paste

Sea salt

1. In a large pot over medium heat, combine the mushrooms, garlic, kombu, onion, celery, carrot, and water. Bring to a simmer and cook for 30 minutes.

2. Remove the pot from the heat and strain the broth through a fine-mesh sieve set over a bowl. Discard or compost the vegetables. If any sediment remains from the dried mushrooms, line the sieve with a paper coffee filter and strain the broth again.

3. Whisk the miso into the broth. Taste and season with salt, as needed.

4. Use the broth or chill and refrigerate in a covered container for up to 3 days, or freeze for up to 3 months.

SUBSTITUTE IT! Use fresh button mushrooms instead of dried shiitakes. Better yet, save mushroom stems over several weeks and keep them frozen until you have at least 1 cup.

Per Serving (1 cup): Total calories: 34; Total fat: 0g; Saturated fat: 0g; Carbohydrates: 7g; Sodium: 359mg; Fiber: 1g; Protein: 1g

FISH STOCK

Dairy-Free
Gluten-Free
Makes:
2 quarts
Prep time:
10 minutes
Cook time:
35 minutes

More than a base for soup or stew, use this stock for poaching fish or for making seafood risotto. Skip the fish oil supplements and choose a fish stock—high fish consumption correlates with reduced risk of depression in epidemiological studies. Choose smaller fish for the least exposure to oceanic pollutants, such as mercury.

2 pounds fresh fish bones, trimmings, and heads

4 fresh parsley stems

1 onion, quartered

1 celery stalk, cut into 2-inch pieces

1 teaspoon peppercorns

½ cup dry white wine

2 quarts water

Sea salt

1. In a large pot over medium-high heat, combine the bones, parsley, onion, celery, peppercorns, white wine, and water. Bring to a gentle simmer, then reduce the heat to medium-low and simmer the stock for 30 minutes. Do not allow it to boil vigorously. Skim the surface of any foam that rises.

2. Taste and season the broth with salt.

3. Strain the broth through a fine-mesh sieve set over a bowl. Discard or compost the fish and vegetables.

4. Use the broth or chill and refrigerate in a covered container for up to 2 days, or freeze for up to 1 month.

PREP TIP Ask your fishmonger to save extra pieces for you, such as heads, tails, and bones, or purchase a whole fish and cut it up yourself.

Per Serving (1 cup): Total calories: 17; Total fat: 0g; Saturated fat: 0g; Carbohydrates: 2g; Sodium: 6mg; Fiber: 0g; Protein: 0g

CHICKEN BROTH

Dairy-Free
Easy Prep
Gluten-Free

Makes:
4 quarts

Prep time:
10 minutes

Cook time:
1 hour, 15 minutes

Chicken broth can clear nasal passages and reduce inflammation. Load up your pot with chicken noodle soup ingredients to not only add depth of flavor, but also reinforce nutrition. As a plus, this recipe yields a good portion of cooked chicken.

1 small (about 3-pound) whole chicken

2 carrots, cut into 2-inch pieces

2 celery stalks, cut into 2-inch pieces

1 onion, quartered

2 garlic cloves, smashed

1 thyme sprig

1 teaspoon peppercorns

1 bay leaf

4 quarts cold water

1 teaspoon sea salt

1. In a large pot over medium-high heat, combine the chicken, carrots, celery, onion, garlic, thyme, peppercorns, bay leaf, water, and salt. Bring to a simmer. Reduce the heat to medium-low and simmer for 45 to 60 minutes. Skim the surface of any foam that rises.

2. When the chicken is cooked through, transfer it to a cutting board. Save for another use.

3. Simmer the broth for 15 minutes more, then strain it through a fine-mesh sieve set over a bowl. Discard or compost the vegetables.

4. Use the broth or chill and refrigerate in a covered container for up to 3 days, or freeze for up to 1 month.

SIMPLIFY IT! Use a rotisserie chicken. Strip most of the meat from the bones and use the chicken carcass to make the broth. Skip step 3 and simmer for a total of 60 to 75 minutes, or until the broth reaches your desired flavor.

Per Serving (1 cup): Total calories: 26; Total fat: 1g; Saturated fat: 0g; Carbohydrates: 2g; Sodium: 158mg; Fiber: 1g; Protein: 2g

GOLDEN MILK

Dairy-Free
Easy Prep
Gluten-Free
Vegan
Makes:
about 3 cups
Prep time:
5 minutes
Cook time:
5 minutes

Turmeric is a potent weapon against all cancers and is the star ingredient in this soup. There's no need to go out and purchase turmeric root—though feel free to, if you like—because the ground version provides the same level of nutrition and even better flavor. Of all the broths that are instantly sippable, this one steals the show. It's intended to be enjoyed as a hot beverage, but you can certainly use it in a soup, such as Cauliflower Curry (page 95).

1 (14-ounce) can light coconut milk

2 teaspoons ground turmeric

½-inch piece fresh ginger

1 cup unsweetened plain almond milk

1 teaspoon peppercorns

Pinch ground cinnamon

1. In a small pot over medium-low heat, combine the coconut milk, almond milk, turmeric, peppercorns, ginger, and cinnamon. Whisk to integrate the turmeric. Bring the liquid to nearly a simmer and cook for 5 minutes.

2. Remove the pan from the heat, cover, and steep the mixture for 5 minutes.

3. Strain the liquid through a fine-mesh sieve set over a bowl, discarding the ginger and peppercorns. Enjoy immediately or chill and refrigerate in a covered container for up to 2 days.

SUBSTITUTE IT! To make this with fresh turmeric, choose a 2-inch piece of turmeric and cut it into ½-inch pieces. Prepare the recipe as directed, discarding the turmeric pieces along with the ginger and peppercorns.

Per Serving (1 cup): Total calories: 122; Total fat: 10g; Saturated fat: 7g; Carbohydrates: 4g; Sodium: 43mg; Fiber: 1g; Protein: 1g

**Mushroom Broth,
top (page 6),
Golden Milk**

Spicy Watermelon
Gazpacho, page 17

CHAPTER TWO

Cold Soups

Sweltering weather calls for delicious chilled soup to nourish and cool you. Because many superfoods offer the greatest nutrition when raw, cold soups are a perfect vehicle for antioxidants, phytochemicals, and heat-sensitive vitamins, such as vitamin C.

This chapter offers some familiar cold soups, such as Tomato Herb Gazpacho (page 16) and Creamy Avocado Soup with Orange-Pepper Salsa (page 20), along with more unusual offerings, including Kale Consommé with Sushi Rice and Seaweed (page 26) or Hibiscus Tea and Ginger Broth with Bok Choy (page 28). Don't worry, though—all ingredients are easy to find.

The great thing about chilled soups is that you can make many of them ahead and simply serve when the mood strikes. One thing to note when preparing these soups —or, really, any food—ahead of time: Don't add acidic ingredients to delicate herbs or vegetables until you're nearly ready to serve. What's great for pickles isn't so great for soup; cilantro will turn brown and onions will lose their punch.

TOMATO HERB GAZPACHO

Dairy-Free
Gluten-Free
Vegan
Serves: 6
Prep time:
20 minutes

Of all the cold soups that come to mind, gazpacho is at the top of my list. This version prominently features fresh herbs—particularly basil, oregano, and thyme. A 2017 study observed that these herbs have many potent antibacterial, antiparasitic, and antifungal compounds that may be beneficial as drug-resistant bacteria become more prevalent. The addition of extra-virgin olive oil helps ensure absorption of the nutrients from the herbs and tomatoes.

- 6 cups roughly chopped heirloom tomatoes
- 2 cucumbers, peeled and diced, divided
- ½ small red onion, diced, divided
- 1 cup loosely packed fresh basil
- ¼ cup loosely packed fresh parsley
- 2 oregano sprigs
- 2 thyme sprigs, leaves only
- ¼ cup extra-virgin olive oil
- 2 tablespoons red wine vinegar
- Sea salt
- Freshly ground pepper

1. In a blender, combine the tomatoes, half the cucumbers, half the red onion, the basil, parsley, oregano, and thyme. Blend until just integrated. The herbs should still be visible.

2. Add the olive oil and vinegar and season with salt and pepper. Blend once or twice, just to combine.

3. Stir in the remaining cucumber and red onion.

PREP TIP To make this soup ahead of time, place all the ingredients, except the vinegar, into the blender and refrigerate for up to 2 days. Add the vinegar and blend before serving.

Per Serving: Total calories: 133; Total fat: 10g; Saturated fat: 1g; Carbohydrates: 11g; Sodium: 20mg; Fiber: 3g; Protein: 2g

SPICY WATERMELON GAZPACHO

Dairy-Free
Easy Prep
Gluten-Free
Vegan
Makes:
2 quarts
Prep time:
20 minutes

Watermelon deserves more superfood credit than it gets. It contains a powerful compound called citrulline. Clinical trials have demonstrated that citrulline improves blood flow and can result in better performance in the gym—and the bedroom. Those are some pretty great benefits from a fruit that's already pretty delicious. In this recipe, the watermelon is paired with tomatoes and spicy serrano chiles.

4 cups
cubed watermelon

4 cups diced
cored tomatoes

1 cucumber, peeled
and diced

½ to 1 serrano chile

½ small red
onion, diced

2 tablespoons red
wine vinegar

2 tablespoons
extra-virgin
olive oil

Sea salt

1. In a blender, combine the watermelon, tomatoes, cucumber, chile, red onion, vinegar, and olive oil. Season with salt. Pulse a few times until somewhat smooth, though some chunks should remain.

2. Serve immediately or chill in the blender for 30 minutes. Blend for 1 second before dividing among serving bowls.

POWER UP! For even more citrulline, choose yellow watermelon, which has four times the amount of the phytochemical than red varieties.

Per Serving (1 cup): Total calories: 77; Total fat: 4g; Saturated fat: 1g; Carbohydrates: 11g; Sodium: 10mg; Fiber: 2g; Protein: 1g

WHITE GAZPACHO WITH GRAPES AND ALMONDS

Dairy-Free
Gluten-Free
Vegan
Makes: 2 quarts
Prep time:
15 minutes
Chill time:
30 minutes

This creamy soup has a plant-based secret—it's not made with heavy cream. Instead, it uses almonds, which garner superfood status in most health food circles. The popular tree nut has been shown to reduce LDL (bad) cholesterol while maintaining HDL (good) cholesterol in numerous studies. Use chilled ingredients so you don't have to chill the soup before serving. I prefer it cold instead of at room temperature.

2 cucumbers, peeled and diced, divided

3 cups halved green grapes, divided

2 garlic cloves, minced

1¼ cups slivered almonds, divided

1 to 2 cups water

¼ cup extra-virgin olive oil

1 tablespoon sherry vinegar

Sea salt

Freshly ground pepper

4 chive sprigs

1. In a blender, combine half the cucumbers, 2 cups of grapes, the garlic, 1 cup of almonds, and 1 cup of water. Puree until completely smooth, adding additional water if needed to reach your desired consistency.

2. Add the olive oil and vinegar and pulse once or twice, just until integrated.

3. Stir in the remaining cucumber, grapes, and almonds. Season with salt and pepper. Chill for 30 minutes before serving. Divide among serving bowls and garnish with chives.

4. Refrigerate leftovers in an airtight container for up to 3 days.

TASTE TIP Before adding the remaining ¼ cup of almonds in step 3, toast them in a dry sauté pan or skillet over medium heat for 3 to 4 minutes, or until gently browned, for added flavor.

Per Serving (1 cup): Total calories: 188; Total fat: 15g; Saturated fat: 2g; Carbohydrates: 11g; Sodium: 3mg; Fiber: 3g; Protein: 4g

CREAMY AVOCADO SOUP WITH ORANGE-PEPPER SALSA

Dairy-Free
Gluten-Free
Vegan
Serves: 4
Prep time:
15 minutes

The superfood ingredients in this flavorful soup work synergistically. Red bell pepper and orange are excellent sources of the carotenoid beta-cryptoxanthin, which has been shown to reduce abdominal fat. And, according to multiple studies, avocado can quadruple the absorption of these and other beneficial carotenoids found in fruits and vegetables.

For the orange-pepper salsa

1 red bell pepper, cored and diced

1 orange, peeled and segmented

½ cup finely diced fresh cilantro

½ jalapeño pepper, minced

Juice of 1 lime

For the creamy avocado soup

3 large ripe avocados, halved and pitted

1 cucumber, peeled and roughly chopped

1 celery stalk, roughly chopped

½ cup roughly chopped fresh cilantro

1 teaspoon ground coriander

1 teaspoon sea salt

Juice of 1 lime

½ teaspoon grated orange zest

2 cups water

To make the orange-pepper salsa

In a medium bowl, combine the red bell pepper, orange segments and accumulated juices, cilantro, jalapeño, and lime juice. Gently toss to mix. Set aside.

To make the creamy avocado soup

1. In a blender, combine the avocado, cucumber, celery, cilantro, coriander, sea salt, lime juice, orange zest, and water. Puree until completely smooth.

2. Divide the soup among serving bowls and top with the salsa. This soup is best enjoyed immediately.

PREP TIP After removing the orange zest for the soup, cut off each end of the orange. Stand the orange on one end on a cutting board. Using a sharp knife, cut the peel away from the flesh. Then, holding the orange in one hand and working over a bowl to catch the juices, carefully slice between each segment and the membrane to remove the flesh. Give the membranes a good squeeze to get all the flavorful juices.

Per Serving: Total calories: 285; Total fat: 22g; Saturated fat: 3g; Carbohydrates: 21g; Sodium: 611mg; Fiber: 13g; Protein: 5g

COCONUT AND SWEET CORN SOUP

Dairy-Free
Gluten-Free
Vegan
Serves: 4
Prep time:
20 minutes
Chill time:
30 minutes

This creamy vegan soup is light enough for a hot summer supper and filling enough to make a complete meal. I opt for plant-based meals often because research shows that simply swapping your protein from meat to plants can reduce the amount of advanced glycation end-products, aptly named "AGEs," that you ingest. As their name suggests, AGEs are responsible for both visible aging—lines and wrinkles—and the aging of your cells and vascular system. Prepare this soup when tomatoes and corn are at their peak for the greatest antioxidant benefit.

3 ears corn, kernels cut from the cobs

1 pound yellow tomatoes, halved, divided

1 shallot, diced

1½ cups canned white beans, rinsed and drained

1 teaspoon sea salt

1 cup light coconut milk

2 tablespoons white wine vinegar

1 tablespoon freshly squeezed lemon juice

Pinch cayenne pepper

1. Reserve ½ cup of corn and ½ cup of tomatoes.

2. In a blender, combine the remaining corn, remaining tomatoes, the shallot, beans, salt, coconut milk, vinegar, lemon juice, and cayenne. Puree until completely smooth. Chill the soup for 30 minutes, or up to 2 hours before serving.

3. Blend for 1 second before serving, just to integrate. Divide the soup among serving bowls and top with the reserved corn and tomatoes.

TASTE TIP As Samin Nosrat has famously highlighted, salt, fat, acid, and heat are the building blocks of flavor. If one is out of balance, food will only taste "okay." When you're making this soup, or any other recipe in this book, just a few drops of vinegar, a few teaspoons of olive oil, or another pinch of salt can take a soup from bland to extraordinary.

Per Serving: Total calories: 216; Total fat: 5g; Saturated fat: 3g; Carbohydrates: 36g; Sodium: 593mg; Fiber: 7g; Protein: 9g

WATERCRESS PUREE

Gluten-Free
Vegetarian
Serves: 4
Prep time:
5 minutes
Cook time:
10 minutes

The Aggregate Nutrient Density Index, ANDI, ranks foods according to how many micronutrients they contain versus how many calories they contain. Watercress is at the top of the scale with a score of 1,000. Watercress is rich in vitamins A, C, E; folate; calcium; and iron. Watercress has a peppery, almost bitter, taste. It is balanced in this soup by onion and vegetable broth. Serve with a dollop of crème fraîche or yogurt.

2 tablespoons
extra-virgin
olive oil

1 yellow onion, diced

1 leek, cleaned well
and cut into slices,
white and pale
green parts only

2 bunches watercress,
tough stem
ends removed

1 quart Superfood
Vegetable Broth
(page 2)

1 tablespoon white
wine vinegar

1 cup whole-milk
yogurt, or
unsweetened
plant-based yogurt

Sea salt

1. In a medium pot over medium heat, heat the olive oil. Add the onion and leek and cook for about 10 minutes until soft. Transfer the cooked vegetables to a blender.

2. Add the watercress, vegetable broth, and vinegar. Puree until very smooth.

3. Add the yogurt and pulse until just integrated. Taste and season with salt. Serve immediately.

SUBSTITUTE IT! If you don't care for the taste of watercress, use spinach and parsley in this soup.

Per Serving: Total calories: 135; Total fat: 9g; Saturated fat: 2g; Carbohydrates: 11g; Sodium: 203mg; Fiber: 2g; Protein: 5g

CHILLED PEA SOUP WITH FRESH HERBS

Dairy-Free
Easy Prep
Gluten-Free
Vegan
Serves: 4
Prep time:
15 minutes
Chill time:
30 minutes

Peas are an unassuming source of plant protein—one cup of peas has 8 grams. It's also a great source of fiber—7 grams per cup. Steak may have protein, but it's got nothing on peas' fiber game. Even better, peas and other legumes and nuts contain phytates, which help the body detox excess iron, a real concern for people who consume heme iron from animal foods.

2 cups shelled fresh peas, or frozen peas, thawed

2 scallions, ends trimmed

8 parsley sprigs, tough stems removed

2 basil sprigs, tough stems removed

1 mint sprig, leaves only, plus more for garnish

2 cups Superfood Vegetable Broth (page 2)

1 tablespoon white wine vinegar

¼ cup extra-virgin olive oil

Sea salt

Freshly ground black pepper

1. In a blender, combine the peas, scallions, parsley, basil, mint, vegetable broth, and vinegar. Puree until very smooth.

2. With the blender running, drizzle in the olive oil. Taste and season with salt and pepper. Chill for 30 minutes before serving, or cover and refrigerate for up to 3 days.

PREP TIP If you can get your hands on fresh peas in spring, they make this soup extra special. Blanch them in boiling water for 2 minutes before adding them to the blender.

Per Serving: Total calories: 184; Total fat: 14g; Saturated fat: 2g; Carbohydrates: 12g; Sodium: 161mg; Fiber: 4g; Protein: 5g

KALE CONSOMMÉ WITH SUSHI RICE AND SEAWEED

Dairy-Free
Gluten-Free
Vegan
Serves: 4
Prep time:
10 minutes
Cook time:
25 minutes

Kale juice is a powerful antidote to high cholesterol and an excellent source of antioxidants. It takes a savory turn in this broth topped with sushi rice and crumbled seaweed. A consommé is technically a soup made with concentrated stock, clarified for a clear appearance—I think the concept is present here. The kale, celery, onion, garlic, and lemon make a refreshing broth without the fiber present in the vegetables, for a clearer appearance than if you simply blended them.

¾ cup short-grain brown rice

1½ cups water

Sea salt

1 bunch kale

1 celery stalk

1 scallion

1 small garlic clove

½ lemon

½ teaspoon rice vinegar

1 sheet nori, toasted

1 teaspoon togarashi (optional)

1. In a medium pot over medium-high heat, combine the rice and water. Generously season with salt. Bring to a gentle simmer. Reduce the heat to low, cover the pot, and cook for 25 minutes, or until all the liquid is absorbed and the rice is cooked through. Let cool to room temperature—do not fluff with a fork!

2. Meanwhile, run the kale, celery, scallion, garlic, and lemon through a juicer. Divide the kale juice among shallow serving bowls.

3. Sprinkle the vinegar over the cooked rice. Divide the rice among the bowls. Crumble the nori over each bowl and season with togarashi (if using).

PREP TIP This soup lends itself to an artful presentation. If you have ring molds, place them in the center of each bowl to form the rice. Alternatively, use a drinking glass to cut out circular shapes from the rice and carefully transfer them to the soup.

Per Serving: Total calories: 191; Total fat: 2g; Saturated fat: 0g; Carbohydrates: 44g; Sodium: 57mg; Fiber: 5g; Protein: 7g

HIBISCUS TEA AND GINGER BROTH WITH BOK CHOY

Dairy-Free
Gluten-Free
Vegan
Serves: 4
Prep time:
15 minutes
Cook time:
10 minutes|
**Steep and chill
time:** 20+ minutes

Green tea gets all the glory, but it should really belong to hibiscus tea, which contains even more antioxidants. It has powerful blood pressure–lowering properties, even when pitted against leading blood pressure medications. That said, you do have to drink a lot of it to see the benefits—this soup gets you off to a good start. The garlic, ginger, maple syrup, and soy sauce beautifully balance hibiscus's tartness.

2 quarts water

4 hibiscus tea bags

1 large garlic
    clove, smashed

1-inch piece
    fresh ginger,
    halved lengthwise

4 ounces thin brown
    rice noodles

2 tablespoons
    low-sodium,
    gluten-free
    soy sauce

1 teaspoon
    maple syrup

2 heads baby bok
    choy, shredded

2 scallions, thinly
    sliced, green
    parts only

1 tablespoon toasted
    sesame oil

1. In a medium pot over high heat, heat the water just to a boil. As soon as it boils, remove the pot from the heat. Add the tea bags, garlic, and ginger. Steep for 10 minutes. Remove and discard the tea bags, garlic, and ginger.

2. Place the rice noodles in a heatproof dish and cover with the hibiscus broth. Transfer the dish to the refrigerator. Cool the noodles for 10 minutes, or until they are soft.

3. Stir in the soy sauce and maple syrup. Transfer the noodles from the broth to a separate container and refrigerate both broth and noodles until the broth is fully chilled.

4. Divide the noodles among serving dishes and ladle the broth around them. Top with the shredded bok choy, scallions, and a drizzle of sesame oil.

SIMPLIFY IT! Make this recipe ready right away. Heat just 1 quart of water in step 1 and proceed through step 2, placing the noodles in the broth and allowing them to soften. Divide them between serving bowls. Add 4 cups of crushed ice to the broth to cool it immediately.

Per Serving: Total calories: 145; Total fat: 4g; Saturated fat: 1g; Carbohydrates: 25g; Sodium: 173mg; Fiber: 3g; Protein: 3g

CHILLED BORSCHT

Easy Prep
Gluten-Free
Vegetarian
Serves: 4
Prep time:
10 minutes
Cook time:
15 minutes
Chill time:
2 hours

Beets have a strong, earthy flavor that's off-putting to some people, but those aromatic compounds are the secret to this subtly sweet superfood. Beets have emerged as a promising source of nitric oxide, which may play a therapeutic role in the prevention and treatment of cardiovascular disease. One reason for this is that nitric oxide relaxes your arteries for greater blood flow. This soup begins with a base of beet juice. If you don't have a juicer, see the Prep Tip.

1 bunch beets (3), peeled, greens reserved for another use

2 cups Superfood Vegetable Broth (page 2), or water

½ cup whole-milk yogurt

1 teaspoon white wine vinegar

Sea salt

4 radishes, trimmed and finely diced

4 scallions, white and green parts, thinly sliced

1 English cucumber, diced

2 tablespoons minced fresh dill, divided

Freshly ground black pepper

1. Run 2 of the beets through a juicer. Transfer the juice to a medium bowl and whisk in the vegetable broth, yogurt, and vinegar. Taste and season with salt.

2. Bring a large pot of salted water to a boil over high heat. Cook the remaining beet for 15 minutes, or until tender. Remove and let cool. When cool enough to handle, cut the beet into small dice.

3. In a large pitcher or non-reactive container, combine the radishes, scallions, cucumber, and 1 tablespoon of the dill. Add the beet juice and diced beet. Chill for at least 2 hours.

4. Divide the soup between serving bowls or refrigerate, covered, overnight. Serve with the remaining dill and season with black pepper.

PREP TIP If you don't have a juicer, dice the beets and place them into a blender with the broth. Puree until completely smooth. Press the mixture through a fine-mesh sieve or a nut milk bag set over a bowl. Be aware, the beets will stain whatever they touch!

Per Serving: Total calories: 69; Total fat: 1g; Saturated fat: 1g; Carbohydrates: 12g; Sodium: 145mg; Fiber: 3g; Protein: 4g

**Cream of Pistachio
Soup with Toasted
Pistachio Dukkah,
page 58**

CHAPTER THREE

Comfort Blends

If you visit the grocery store, you'll probably find a total of three pureed soups available—tomato, sweet potato, and butternut squash. I adore all three, but sometimes it's nice to have a little variety. This chapter features everything—from the familiar Tomato Basil Soup (page 46) to a Parsnip Chestnut Bisque with Pomegranate Hazelnut Pesto (page 40)—for comfort foods that will quickly become favorites.

One of the benefits of pureed soups is that the nutrients are more bioavailable. Let's face it—we don't always do the best job of chewing. That means that some of the healthy foods we fill our plates with never have the chance to provide the health benefits we're after because larger pieces of food pass through us not fully digested. I once heard someone say, "Your stomach doesn't have teeth." It really stuck with me. If you want all the benefits of that kale salad, chew it. Or, in this case, puree it!

SWEET POTATO COCONUT CURRY

Dairy-Free
Easy Prep
Gluten-Free
Vegan
Serves: 4
Prep time:
15 minutes
Cook time:
25 minutes

The Center for Science in the Public Interest ranks sweet potatoes as one of the top 10 best foods you can eat. That's generous praise for the humble and inexpensive root vegetable, but sweet potatoes deserve it. They're loaded with carotenoids, vitamin C, and fiber and have far more potassium than even bananas. This soup maximizes the effectiveness of all these awesome micronutrients with full-fat coconut milk, which improves their absorption. As an added bonus, the turmeric in the curry powder is a potent cancer fighter.

1 tablespoon coconut oil, or canola oil

1 yellow onion, diced

2 garlic cloves, smashed

¼-inch piece fresh ginger

¼ teaspoon red pepper flakes

4 cups diced peeled sweet potato

1 quart Superfood Vegetable Broth (page 2)

1 cup full-fat coconut milk

2 tablespoons curry powder

1 teaspoon garam masala

Sea salt

1 lime, halved

1. In a large pot over medium heat, heat the coconut oil. Add the onion and cook for about 5 minutes until somewhat soft. Add the garlic, ginger, and red pepper flakes. Cook for 1 minute more.

2. Stir in the sweet potato, vegetable broth, coconut milk, curry powder, and garam masala. Generously season with salt. Cover the pot and simmer for 15 minutes, or until the sweet potato is soft. Using an immersion blender, puree the soup.

3. Season with a squeeze of lime juice and another a pinch of salt, until it has just the right balance. Serve immediately or cover and refrigerate for up to 3 days.

SIMPLIFY IT! To save time, combine all the ingredients in a slow cooker, cover, and cook on low heat for 4 to 6 hours.

Per Serving: Total calories: 310; Total fat: 15g; Saturated fat: 12g; Carbohydrates: 41g; Sodium: 192mg; Fiber: 7g; Protein: 5g

CHIPOTLE ORANGE SWEET POTATO SOUP

This creamy sweet potato soup has a surprising twist. Spicy, smoky chipotle in adobo sauce and sweet orange juice blend with sweet potatoes for a soup you'll fall in love with.

2 quarts Superfood Vegetable Broth (page 2)

6 cups diced peeled sweet potato

1 canned chipotle in adobo sauce, minced

1 to 3 teaspoons adobo sauce (from the can)

1 teaspoon smoked paprika

½ cup freshly squeezed orange juice, or 1½ tablespoons orange juice concentrate

½ teaspoon sea salt

2 tablespoons cultured butter, or vegan butter

1. In a large pot over medium heat, stir together the vegetable broth, sweet potato, chipotle, 1 teaspoon of adobo sauce, the paprika, orange juice, and salt. Bring to a simmer, cover the pot, and cook for about 15 minutes, until the sweet potato is tender.

2. Add the butter. Using an immersion blender, puree the soup. Taste and add additional adobo sauce, if desired. Serve immediately or cover and refrigerate for up to 3 days.

SUBSTITUTE IT! Cultured butter adds probiotics and fat to improve the nutrient absorption rate. If you prefer a dairy-free or fat-free soup, skip it.

Per Serving: Total calories: 298; Total fat: 6g; Saturated fat: 4g; Carbohydrates: 56g; Sodium: 664mg; Fiber: 8g; Protein: 6g

ROASTED PUMPKIN SOUP WITH YOGURT AND PEPITAS

Dairy-Free
Gluten-Free
Vegan
Serves: 4
Prep time:
15 minutes
Cook time:
55 minutes

This soup may help you live longer. It's a bold claim, but a study published in 2011 looked at blood concentrations of α-carotene—the primary carotenoid in pumpkin—and found that it was inversely associated with risk of death from all causes. That means the more fruits and vegetables with α-carotene that people were eating, the higher their blood levels of the micronutrient were, and the less likely they were to die prematurely. Top off your bowl with pumpkin seeds and a swirl of plant-based yogurt for a nice contrast of texture and flavor.

1 small (about 5-pounds) pumpkin, peeled, seeded, and diced

3 tablespoons canola oil, divided

2 tablespoons Cajun spice blend

1 teaspoon sea salt

1 yellow onion, diced

2 garlic cloves, minced

1 quart Superfood Vegetable Broth (page 2)

½ teaspoon apple cider vinegar

1 cup unsweetened plain plant-based milk

6 ounces unsweetened plain non-dairy yogurt

¼ cup pepitas

1. Preheat the oven to 375°F.

2. Spread the pumpkin cubes onto a rimmed sheet pan. Drizzle with 2 tablespoons of canola oil and toss to coat. Season with the Cajun spice blend and sea salt.

3. Roast the pumpkin for 35 to 45 minutes, or until tender and beginning to brown.

Continued ▶

4. Meanwhile, in a large pot over medium heat, heat the remaining 1 tablespoon of canola oil. Add the onion and garlic. Cook for 5 minutes until soft and fragrant.

5. When the pumpkin is done, add it to the pot along with the vegetable broth, vinegar, and milk. Bring to a simmer and cook for 5 minutes.

6. Using an immersion blender, puree the soup. Taste and season with more salt, as needed.

7. Divide the soup among serving bowls. Drizzle each with the yogurt and a sprinkle of pepitas. Serve immediately or cover and refrigerate for up to 3 days.

TASTE TIP Toast the pepitas in a dry sauté pan or skillet over medium heat for about 3 minutes until slightly dried out but not quite browned.

Per Serving: Total calories: 540; Total fat: 18g; Saturated fat: 3g; Carbohydrates: 89g; Sodium: 2,171mg; Fiber: 31g; Protein: 16g

CREAMY CAULIFLOWER SOUP

Dairy-Free
Easy Prep
Gluten-Free
Vegan
Serves: 4
Prep time:
5 minutes
Cook time:
15 minutes

Cauliflower, like other cruciferous vegetables, can help prevent DNA damage. This is especially important if you engage in any activities that cause oxidative stress—such as eating meat, exercising, feeling overwhelmed, encountering environmental pollutants, exposure to the sun . . . you know, living! DNA damage can result in the development of a variety of cancers, so it's important to counteract oxidative stress with the antioxidants found in plants.

1 head cauliflower, broken into florets

2 garlic cloves, peeled

2 cups Superfood Vegetable Broth (page 2)

2 cups plant-based milk

3 tablespoons vegan butter

½ teaspoon sea salt

1. In a large pot over medium heat, combine the cauliflower, garlic, and vegetable broth. Cover the pot and bring to a simmer. Cook for 10 minutes.

2. Stir in the milk, butter, and salt.

3. Using an immersion blender, puree the soup until smooth. Serve immediately or cover and refrigerate for up to 3 days.

TASTE TIP For a slightly cheesy flavor without adding dairy, stir in 2 tablespoons nutritional yeast in step 2.

Per Serving: Total calories: 133; Total fat: 10g; Saturated fat: 3g; Carbohydrates: 10g; Sodium: 565mg; Fiber: 4g; Protein: 4g

PARSNIP CHESTNUT BISQUE WITH POMEGRANATE HAZELNUT PESTO

Gluten-Free

Vegetarian

Serves: 6

Prep time:
20 minutes

Cook time:
30 minutes

This creamy parsnip and chestnut soup is a quintessential fall and winter dish. Parsnips and pomegranates are at their peak during this season. Pomegranate deserves its superfood status. Just type it into the leading medical journal database and you'll find numerous articles on its ability to fight cancer, lower blood pressure, and fight inflammation. Unfortunately, there aren't many recipes calling for pomegranate, and a pasteurized juice may not provide all the benefits of fresh pomegranate. Using it in a loose pesto, as in this recipe, is a delicious way to sneak it into your diet.

For the pesto

1 cup
pomegranate arils

¼ cup finely chopped
toasted hazelnuts

¼ cup minced fresh
flat-leaf parsley

2 tablespoons
minced fresh mint

2 tablespoons
extra-virgin
olive oil

Grated zest of 1 lime

Juice of 1 lime

Sea salt

For the bisque

1 tablespoon
extra-virgin
olive oil

1 small yellow onion,
cut into slices

1 pound parsnips,
peeled
and chopped

2 quarts Superfood
Vegetable Broth
(page 2)

5 ounces roasted,
peeled chestnuts

1 teaspoon sea
salt, plus more
as needed

¼ cup sour cream,
or vegan
sour cream

To make the pesto

In a medium bowl, stir together the pomegranate arils, hazelnuts, parsley, mint, olive oil, lime zest, and lime juice. Taste and season with salt.

To make the bisque

1. In a large pot over medium heat, heat the olive oil. Add the onion and cook for about 8 minutes, until mostly soft. Add the parsnips and cook for 5 minutes more.

2. Add the vegetable broth, chestnuts, and salt. Bring the soup to a simmer. Cook, uncovered, for 10 to 12 minutes, or until the parsnips are soft.

3. When the parsnips are tender, stir the sour cream into the soup.

4. Using an immersion blender, puree the soup until smooth. Taste and season with additional salt, as needed.

5. Divide the soup among serving bowls. Top with the pomegranate hazelnut pesto.

6. Refrigerate cooled leftovers separately in airtight containers for about 3 days.

PREP TIP Although chestnuts are readily available in most grocery stores during the holidays, they can be difficult to source the rest of the year. In the off-season, save yourself the frustration and order them online.

Per Serving: Total calories: 244; Total fat: 13g; Saturated fat: 3g; Carbohydrates: 30g; Sodium: 618mg; Fiber: 6g; Protein: 5g

CREAMY ASPARAGUS AND HERB SOUP

Dairy-Free
Easy Prep
Gluten-Free
Vegan
Serve: 4
Prep time: 10 minutes
Cook time: 15 minutes

So many superfoods get their superpowers from antioxidants, including asparagus. The strongly flavored vegetable is credited with improving reproductive health and hormone balance by reducing oxidative stress and increasing antioxidant levels in the body. This light and refreshing vegetable soup packs two bunches of asparagus and six cups of green peas into it. They're enlivened with fragrant lemon zest and fresh tarragon. Olive oil gives the soup body and improves the absorption of the nutrients in the vegetables without employing heavy cream.

4 tablespoons extra-virgin olive oil, divided

1 large leek, cleaned well and cut into slices

1 small garlic clove, minced

6 cups frozen green peas, thawed

2 bunches asparagus, tough woody ends removed

2 quarts Superfood Vegetable Broth (page 2)

½ teaspoon finely grated lemon zest

½ cup roughly chopped fresh flat-leaf parsley

1 tablespoon minced fresh tarragon

1 teaspoon white wine vinegar

Sea salt

1. In a large pot over medium heat, heat 1 tablespoon of the olive oil. Add the leek and cook for about 5 minutes until just softened. Add the garlic and cook for 30 seconds more.

2. Add the peas, asparagus, vegetable broth, and lemon zest. Bring the soup to a simmer and cook for about 3 minutes until the asparagus is bright green.

3. Stir in the parsley, tarragon, and vinegar.

4. Carefully transfer two-thirds of the soup to a blender. Vent the lid and cover it loosely with a kitchen towel. Blend the soup on low speed until very smooth.

5. Add the remaining 3 tablespoons of olive oil and season with salt to taste. Transfer the pureed soup back to the pot and stir to combine. Serve immediately or cover and refrigerate for up to 3 days.

PREP TIP Save a handful of the asparagus tips from step 2 to garnish the soup when serving. They add a nice textural contrast to the creamy soup.

Per Serving: Total calories: 378; Total fat: 15g; Saturated fat: 2g; Carbohydrates: 48g; Sodium: 568mg; Fiber: 17g; Protein: 19g

GINGER BEET SOUP WITH CITRUS AND GREEK YOGURT

Gluten-Free
Vegetarian
Serves: 4
Prep time:
10 minute
Cook time:
20 minutes

Ever since I began reading the studies of cyclists, soccer players, kayakers, and other athletes who get their performance-enhancing benefits from beets, I've been a little obsessed. How could such a humble vegetable offer such profound benefits? It turns out it's the nitrates in beets that reduce oxygen demands and improve glucose uptake—meaning you use oxygen and glucose more efficiently for better performance. That said, the findings suggest more than a one-time dose for maximum effect. So, make a batch of this soup and enjoy it for days before your big race!

1 tablespoon extra-virgin olive oil

½ red onion, diced

1 bunch beets (3), trimmed and scrubbed, cut into large chunks

1-inch piece fresh ginger, halved

1 garlic clove, smashed

Grated zest of 1 orange

Juice of 1 orange

2 quarts Superfood Vegetable Broth (page 2)

Sea salt

½ cup plain Greek yogurt

1. In a large pot over medium heat, heat the olive oil. Add the red onion and cook for 5 minutes until it begins to soften. Add the beets, ginger, garlic, orange zest, 2 tablespoons of the orange juice, and the vegetable broth. Bring the soup to a simmer, cover the pot, and cook for 15 minutes, or until the beets are tender.

2. Remove and discard the garlic and ginger.

3. Using an immersion blender, puree the soup until very smooth. Taste and season with salt.

4. Divide the soup among serving bowls and drizzle with the yogurt.

5. Refrigerate cooled leftovers in an airtight container for up to 3 days.

POWER UP! Like other dark leafy greens, beet greens are a good source of phytochemicals, antioxidants, and fiber. Take 4 to 6 of the cleaned beet leaves and stack them on top of each other. Roll into a tight cylinder and thinly slice the roll to make a chiffonade. Stir this into the soup at the end of step 3. Simmer for another minute or two, just until the greens are bright green and wilted.

Per Serving: Total calories: 125; Total fat: 6g; Saturated fat: 2g; Carbohydrates: 16g; Sodium: 373mg; Fiber: 4g; Protein: 5g

TOMATO BASIL SOUP

Dairy-Free
Easy Prep
Gluten-Free
Vegan
Serves: 4
Prep time:
10 minutes
Cook time:
25 minutes

Lycopene is a powerful antioxidant, and it's even more bioavailable from tomatoes when they're cooked. One reason for this is that the cooking process breaks down the tomato's cell walls. Nevertheless, the soup tastes infinitely better if you start with fresh tomatoes. Once you make tomato soup with fresh tomatoes, you'll never go back to canned. There's something about their freshness that you really taste in the soup—even though it's cooked. Unlike many store-bought varieties, this one has no heavy cream but still has a rich, creamy texture.

8 pounds fresh tomatoes, quartered

4 basil sprigs, leaves only

1 teaspoon sea salt

¼ cup extra-virgin olive oil

1. In a large pot over medium heat, combine the tomatoes, basil, salt, and olive oil. Bring to a simmer. Cook for 15 to 20 minutes, until the tomatoes are very soft and mostly broken down.

2. Using an immersion blender, puree the soup to your desired texture. Serve immediately or cover and refrigerate for up to 3 days.

TASTE TIP Skip the pale plum tomatoes in January and go for the best heirloom varieties, if you can. Not only will they offer significantly greater nutritional value, they'll also taste so much better and create a soup that's addictively delicious.

Per Serving: Total calories: 311; Total fat: 17g; Saturated fat: 2g; Carbohydrates: 42g; Sodium: 663mg; Fiber: 10g; Protein: 8g

SUNSHINE VEGETABLE TURMERIC SOUP

Dairy-Free
Gluten-Free
Vegan
Serves: 4
Prep time:
10 minutes
Cook time:
30 minutes

This soup is pure sunshine. The humble vegetable soup is perfect for those cold winter days when the sun isn't shining, and colds and flu wreak havoc. Spicy ginger and pungent garlic bring flavor and immune-boosting powers. A 2014 review observed that these functional ingredients may boost the immune system and offer free radical scavenging and anti-inflammatory properties. That's a lot of goodness in a single bowl.

1 tablespoon coconut oil, or extra-virgin olive oil

1 small yellow onion, diced

1 tablespoon minced peeled fresh ginger

2 garlic cloves, minced

1 tablespoon ground turmeric

½ teaspoon ground coriander

Pinch cayenne pepper

1 large sweet potato, peeled and diced

2 cups cauliflower florets

2 quarts Superfood Vegetable Broth (page 2)

1 cup raw cashews

1 teaspoon sea salt

1 tablespoon freshly squeezed lime juice

1. In a large pot over medium-high heat, heat the coconut oil. Add the onion and cook for 5 minutes until it begins to soften. Add the ginger, garlic, turmeric, coriander, and cayenne and cook for 1 minute more, being careful not to burn the garlic.

2. Add the sweet potato, cauliflower, vegetable broth, cashews, and salt. Bring the soup to a simmer, cover the pot, and cook for 20 minutes.

3. Stir in the lime juice.

Continued ▶

4. Using an immersion blender, puree the soup to your desired texture. Serve immediately or cover and refrigerate for up to 3 days.

TASTE TIP For an even heartier soup, stir in 1 cup full-fat coconut milk at step 3.

Per Serving: Total calories: 301; Total fat: 18g; Saturated fat: 5g; Carbohydrates: 27g; Sodium: 920mg; Fiber: 8g; Protein: 10g

CREAM OF CASHEW PEA SOUP

Dairy-Free
Easy Prep
Gluten-Free
Vegan
Serves: 4
Prep time: 5 minutes
Cook time: 40 minutes

Cashews bring a delicious creaminess to this rich pea soup with flavor from a slow-cooked mixture of onion, celery, garlic, and bright green peas. Cashews are a superfood in their own right, but when compared to heavy cream, they're downright heroic. A 2017 study published in the *American Journal of Clinical Nutrition* found that eating cashews significantly reduced LDL (bad) and total cholesterol. Dairy can't say the same.

3 tablespoons extra-virgin olive oil

1 large yellow onion, diced

2 celery stalks, minced

4 garlic cloves, minced

Sea salt

2 quarts Superfood Vegetable Broth (page 2)

1 cup raw cashews

1 pound frozen green peas

1 tablespoon white wine vinegar

1. In a large pot over medium-low heat, heat the olive oil. Add the onion, celery, and garlic. Generously season with salt. Cook for 20 to 30 minutes, until very soft.

2. Stir in the vegetable broth and cashews. Simmer the soup for 10 minutes.

3. Stir in the peas and vinegar.

4. Using an immersion blender, puree the soup until smooth. Serve immediately or cover and refrigerate for up to 3 days.

POWER UP! Add 1 to 2 tablespoons of white miso paste to this soup in step 3 for a salty, umami boost and a nice dose of probiotics.

Per Serving: Total calories: 400; Total fat: 25g; Saturated fat: 4g; Carbohydrates: 33g; Sodium: 458mg; Fiber: 10g; Protein: 14g

CREAM OF BROCCOLI SOUP WITH LEMON AND CHILI

Easy Prep
Gluten-Free
Serves: 4
Prep time:
5 minutes
Cook time:
20 minutes

Broccoli is the star of the show in this tasty, comforting soup. For maximum nutrition, chop the broccoli about an hour ahead of time. This allows for the production of a heat-resistant phytochemical called sulforaphane, a potent cancer fighter. Don't have time to spare? Buy pre-chopped bags of broccoli at the supermarket.

2 tablespoons
   extra-virgin
   olive oil

2 heads
   broccoli, chopped

¼ teaspoon red
   pepper flakes

4 garlic
   cloves, smashed

Zest of 1 lemon

2 quarts Chicken
   Broth (page 11)

1 cup whole-milk,
   plain yogurt, or
   plant-based yogurt

Sea salt

1. In a large pot over medium heat, heat the olive oil. Add the broccoli and sauté for 2 to 3 minutes, until it begins to turn bright green. Add the red pepper flakes and garlic. Cook for 30 seconds, just until fragrant.

2. Stir in the lemon zest and chicken broth. Bring the soup to a simmer and cook for 15 minutes, or until the broccoli is tender. Remove the soup from the heat.

3. Using an immersion blender, puree the soup until mostly smooth. I like it to retain some texture.

4. Add the yogurt and blend again. Taste and season with salt. Serve immediately or cover and refrigerate for up to 3 days.

PREP TIP Once you get past their tough exterior, broccoli stems are actually quite tender. Use a vegetable peeler to remove the tough, fibrous outer layer, then slice.

Per Serving: Total calories: 176; Total fat: 11g; Saturated fat: 2g; Carbohydrates: 12g; Sodium: 365mg; Fiber: 5g; Protein: 9g

CHIPOTLE BLACK BEAN SOUP

Dairy-Free
Gluten-Free
Vegan
Serves: 4
Prep time:
10 minutes
Cook time:
70 minutes

Black beans have powerful cholesterol-fighting and insulin-lowering properties, making them an excellent plant-based protein for people with metabolic syndrome. But I'll be honest—they can be bland (you can even sneak them into brownies!). Smoky, spicy chipotle peppers in tangy adobo sauce infuse this soup with flavor. Stir in additional adobo sauce at the end, depending on how spicy you like your soup.

2 tablespoons
  extra-virgin
  olive oil

2 celery
  stalks, minced

2 carrots, diced

1 yellow
  onion, minced

1 red bell
  pepper, diced

4 garlic
  cloves, minced

1½ cups dried
  black beans,
  ideally soaked in
  water overnight
  and drained

1 canned chipotle
  pepper in
  adobo, minced

2 teaspoons adobo
  sauce (from
  the can)

1 tablespoon
  ground cumin

1 tablespoon
  smoked paprika

2 quarts Superfood
  Vegetable Broth
  (page 2)

1 tablespoon freshly
  squeezed lime juice

Sea salt

1. In a large pot over medium heat, heat the olive oil. Add the celery, carrots, onion, red bell pepper, and garlic. Cook for 10 minutes, until mostly soft.

2. Stir in the black beans, chipotle pepper, adobo sauce, cumin, paprika, and vegetable broth. Bring the soup to a simmer, partially cover the pot, and cook for 1 hour, or until the beans are soft.

3. Carefully transfer half the soup to a blender, vent the lid, and cover it loosely with a kitchen towel. Puree the soup until smooth. Pour the soup back into the pot.

4. Stir in the lime juice. Taste and season with salt. Serve immediately or cover and refrigerate for up to 3 days.

PREP TIP   To core a bell pepper easily, place it on its side with the stem facing toward you. Place the tip of the knife into the middle of the pepper just to the right side of the stem. Slice through the flesh, rotating the pepper counter-clockwise, allowing the knife to cut in a circular fashion around the stem.

Per Serving: Total calories: 284; Total fat: 9g; Saturated fat: 1g; Carbohydrates: 48g; Sodium: 390mg; Fiber: 13g; Protein: 14g

CREAM OF MUSHROOM SOUP

Gluten-Free
Vegetarian
Serves: 4
Prep time: 10 minutes
Cook time: 35 minutes

Cooking mushrooms in liquid—as opposed to other cooking methods—makes their beta-glucans more bioavailable. Beta-glucans are a form of soluble fiber than can improve vascular health and lower cholesterol. If cream of mushroom soup evokes memories of the stodgy canned variety, prepare to be surprised. The earthy, complex flavors of mushrooms permeate this savory soup.

2 tablespoons extra-virgin olive oil

1 onion, minced

3 garlic cloves, minced

1 teaspoon fresh thyme leaves

1 teaspoon minced fresh rosemary leaves

1 pound assorted mushrooms, cremini, oyster, or shiitake, roughly chopped

¼ cup dry white wine

2 quarts Mushroom Broth (page 6)

1 cup cashews

1 ounce dried wild mushrooms, soaked in hot water

¼ cup sour cream or vegan sour cream

Sea salt

1. In a large pot over medium heat, heat the olive oil. Add the onion, garlic, thyme, and rosemary. Cook for 10 minutes until soft.

2. Add the fresh mushrooms and cook for 5 minutes, stirring frequently.

3. Add the white wine and cook for about 2 minutes until reduced to just a couple tablespoons of liquid.

4. Add the mushroom broth and cashews. Bring the soup to a simmer and cook for 15 minutes.

5. Using an immersion blender, puree the soup until smooth.

6. Drain the wild mushrooms, adding the soaking liquid to the soup (strain out any sediment through a paper coffee filter, if needed). Finely slice the mushrooms and add them to the soup. Cook for 3 minutes.

7. Remove the soup from the heat and stir in the sour cream. Taste and season with salt. Serve immediately, or cover and refrigerate for up to 2 days.

SUBSTITUTE IT! If you don't have time to prepare the mushroom broth ahead, no worries. It's still wonderful using vegetable broth or even chicken broth.

Per Serving: Total calories: 415; Total fat: 28g; Saturated fat: 7g; Carbohydrates: 34g; Sodium: 39mg; Fiber: 6g; Protein: 12g

CREAMY FENNEL
AND CELERIAC SOUP

Gluten-Free
Vegetarian
Serves: 4
Prep time:
20 minutes
Cook time:
25 minutes

Fennel is one of my favorite vegetables. It has a creamy texture and a unique anise flavor that mellows as it cooks. It pairs well with celeriac and potatoes in this smooth soup. Like celeriac and potatoes, fennel has a pale color, which may lead you to think it doesn't offer any nutritional benefits. But, according to research published in 2018, fennel may have mood-boosting and fertility-enhancing properties.

1 tablespoon extra-virgin olive oil

1 leek, cleaned well and thinly sliced, white and pale green parts only

2 fennel bulbs, tough stems removed, cut into chunks, fronds reserved

1 head celeriac, peeled and cut into chunks

2 quarts Superfood Vegetable Broth (page 2)

Sea salt

1 teaspoon white wine

1 cup half-and-half or coconut milk

1. In a large pot over medium heat, heat the olive oil. Add the leek and cook for about 5 minutes, until somewhat soft.

2. Add the fennel, celeriac, and vegetable broth. Season with salt. Bring the soup to a simmer, cover the pot, and cook for 20 minutes, or until the vegetables are completely tender.

3. Stir in the white wine and half-and-half.

4. Using an immersion blender, puree the soup until smooth. Divide among serving bowls and top with the reserved fennel fronds. Alternatively, chill and refrigerate in an airtight container for up to 3 days.

TASTE TIP This soup also makes amazing mashed "potatoes." After step 2, drain the vegetables, discarding the cooking liquid or reserving it for another use. To the vegetables, add ½ cup half-and-half. Mash to your desired consistency, adding more half-and-half only as needed.

Per Serving: Total calories: 196; Total fat: 11g; Saturated fat: 5g; Carbohydrates: 22g; Sodium: 441mg; Fiber: 7g; Protein: 6g

CREAM OF PISTACHIO SOUP
WITH TOASTED PISTACHIO DUKKAH

Gluten-Free
Vegetarian
Serves: 4
Prep time:
15 minutes
Cook time:
30 minutes

Of any nut, pistachios boast the highest levels of vitamins B_6, E, and K; thiamin; phytosterols; xanthophyll carotenoids; copper; iron; and magnesium. Phew, that's a lot for one tiny little nut! They also have exceptional antioxidant and anti-inflammatory potential. In this soup, they're blended with white sweet potatoes for a creamy, jade-colored soup and toasted for a crunchy topping, called *dukkah*. Dukkah is a Middle Eastern condiment of sesame seeds, nuts, herbs, and spices—a last-minute addition to boost flavor and superfoods.

2 tablespoons extra-virgin olive oil

1 leek, cleaned well and thinly sliced, white and pale green parts only

1 small yellow onion, diced

1 teaspoon minced peeled fresh ginger

Sea salt

1 cup diced white sweet potato

1 quart Superfood Vegetable Broth (page 2)

¼ cup white wine

1½ cups shelled pistachios, divided

1 tablespoon cumin seeds

1 teaspoon peppercorns

1 teaspoon fennel seeds

1 teaspoon sea salt

2 tablespoons sesame seeds

1. In a large sauté pan or skillet over medium heat, heat the olive oil. Add the leek, onion, ginger, and a generous pinch of salt. Cook for 10 minutes, or until very soft.

2. Add the sweet potato, vegetable broth, white wine, and 1 cup of pistachios. Bring the soup to a gentle simmer and cook for 12 to 15 minutes, or until the pistachios are soft.

3. Using an immersion blender, puree the soup until very smooth.

4. To make the dukkah, in a large dry skillet over medium heat, toast the remaining ½ cup of pistachios for 4 to 5 minutes until fragrant and dried out a bit. Let cool completely.

5. In a clean spice grinder, combine the cooled pistachios, cumin seeds, peppercorns, fennel seeds, and salt. Pulse a few times until the spices are broken up but not blended to a powder. Stir in the sesame seeds.

6. Divide the soup among serving bowls and sprinkle with some of the dukkah. You might not use all of it; save extras in an airtight container for up to 1 month. Refrigerate leftover soup in an airtight container for up to 3 days.

TASTE TIP For even more flavor, toast the peppercorns, cumin, and fennel in a dry skillet for 2 to 3 minutes and let cool completely before blending.

Per Serving: Total calories: 425; Total fat: 29g; Saturated fat: 4g; Carbohydrates: 31g; Sodium: 1,036mg; Fiber: 8g; Protein: 12g

Ribolitta, page 70

CHAPTER FOUR

Hearty Warmers

Like parents, authors aren't supposed to pick favorites. But I'll let you in on a little secret—this chapter is my favorite. These are the soups I go to again and again. They are more of a meal than the chilled and pureed soups, but lighter than the stews and chilis. The soups in this chapter highlight a diverse array of superfoods, including legumes, vegetables, herbs, and spices. Flavors draw from global cuisines and will bring an immense variety to your soup repertoire. I've been making many of the recipes in this chapter since I learned how while working in restaurants in college.

ROASTED BROCCOLI
AND GARLIC SOUP

Dairy-Free
Gluten-Free
Serves: 4
Prep time:
15 minutes
Cook time:
30 minutes

When roasted, broccoli takes on a new, complex flavor dimension. Like other roasted vegetables, its sugars caramelize, bringing depth to an otherwise simple soup. As in previous broccoli recipes, cut the broccoli at least 45 minutes before preparing this soup to allow the potent phytochemical sulforaphane to develop. The garlic mellows when roasted, becoming almost sweet.

8 cups broccoli florets

6 garlic cloves, unpeeled

3 tablespoons extra-virgin olive oil

Sea salt

Freshly ground black pepper

1 russet potato, peeled and sliced

½ teaspoon lemon zest

¼ teaspoon red pepper flakes

2 quarts Chicken Broth (page 11)

4 cups shredded cooked chicken, from Chicken Broth (optional)

1. Preheat the oven to 400°F.

2. Spread the broccoli and garlic cloves onto a rimmed sheet pan and drizzle with the olive oil. Season with salt and pepper.

3. Roast for 15 to 18 minutes, until the broccoli is deeply browned.

4. When cool enough to handle, carefully peel the garlic cloves. Transfer them and the broccoli to a large pot and add the potato, lemon zest, red pepper flakes, and chicken broth. Place the pot over medium heat and bring the soup to a simmer. Cook for about 10 minutes, until the potato is soft.

5. Stir in the cooked chicken (if using). Serve immediately or cover and refrigerate for up to 2 days.

SUBSTITUTE IT! To make this soup vegan, use Superfood Vegetable Broth (page 2) and stir in 2 teaspoons of white miso in step 4 for a boost of umami flavors and probiotics. Omit the chicken. Add white beans or another plant-based protein source instead.

Per Serving: Total calories: 236; Total fat: 13g; Saturated fat: 2g; Carbohydrates: 20g; Sodium: 357mg; Fiber: 7g; Protein: 7g

WEST AFRICAN PEANUT SOUP

Dairy-Free
Gluten-Free
Vegan
Serves: 4
Prep time:
10 minutes
Cook time:
35 minutes

Creamy, salty peanut butter melds with spicy red pepper flakes, ginger, and garlic in this flavorful soup. The star of the show here: collard greens and their good nitrates. Nitrites in plants significantly reduce cancer risk, whereas processed meats are listed as a class 1 carcinogen.

1 tablespoon
   extra-virgin
   olive oil

1 red onion, minced

2 tablespoons minced
   peeled fresh ginger

1 tablespoon
   minced garlic

¼ teaspoon red
   pepper flakes

1 sweet potato,
   peeled and diced

2 quarts Superfood
   Vegetable Broth
   (page 2)

¾ cup unsalted
   natural
   peanut butter

½ cup tomato paste

1 bunch collard
   greens, stems
   discarded,
   thinly sliced

1. In a large pot over medium heat, heat the olive oil. Add the red onion, ginger, garlic, and red pepper flakes. Cook for about 5 minutes, until the onion begins to soften.

2. Add the sweet potato and vegetable broth. Bring the soup to a simmer and cook for 15 minutes, until the sweet potato is soft.

3. Stir in the peanut butter and tomato paste. Using an immersion blender, puree the soup until smooth.

4. Stir in the collard greens and cook for 10 minutes more until soft. Serve immediately or cover and refrigerate for up to 4 days.

TASTE TIP Top the soup with crushed peanuts and minced fresh cilantro for more texture, flavor, and nutrition.

Per Serving: Total calories: 421; Total fat: 28g; Saturated fat: 4g; Carbohydrates: 34g; Sodium: 582mg; Fiber: 11g; Protein: 17g

MISO VEGETABLE SOUP

Dairy-Free
Vegan
Serves: 4
Prep time:
10 minutes
Cook time:
15 minutes

The elegant simplicity of this traditional Japanese soup is a comforting change of pace. Potato, carrot, broccoli, mushrooms, and cabbage are all quickly cooked in a miso broth, thickened with a bit of tahini. This soup is loaded with probiotics from the miso paste. You can find baked tofu alongside tofu and tempeh in the grocery store.

2 quarts Miso Broth (page 9)

1 large russet potato, peeled and cut into matchsticks

1 large carrot, cut into matchsticks

1 small head broccoli, cut into florets

½ small head green cabbage, thinly sliced

4 ounces fresh shiitake mushrooms, thinly sliced

6 ounces baked tofu, diced

2 tablespoons tahini

1 teaspoon rice vinegar

1. In a large pot over medium-high heat, bring the miso broth to a simmer.

2. Add the potato and cook for 2 minutes. Add the carrot, broccoli, cabbage, and mushrooms. Simmer for 3 minutes.

3. Add the tofu and cook for 2 to 3 minutes.

4. Stir in the tahini and vinegar.

5. Serve immediately or cover and refrigerate for up to 3 days.

SUBSTITUTE IT! You can also use the Kombu Dashi (page 8) in this recipe. Stir in ¼ cup white miso paste just before serving.

Per Serving: Total calories: 337; Total fat: 7g; Saturated fat: 1g; Carbohydrates: 56g; Sodium: 1,030mg; Fiber: 13g; Protein: 19g

CURRIED LENTIL SOUP WITH RED ONION SALSA

Dairy-Free
Gluten-Free
Vegan
Serves: 4
Prep time:
15 minutes
Cook time:
30 minutes

Have you heard of food synergy? It occurs when the compounds in two foods are made even more bioavailable when combined. The idea is that one food has 10 units of antioxidants and another has 10 units of antioxidants but, when combined, they may offer 40 units; they're more than the sum of their parts. That's what happens in this soup—turmeric and red onion have a thing going on! Together, they're a powerful protector against colon cancer.

For the red onion salsa

1 cup minced red onion

1 cup minced fresh cilantro

1 tablespoon freshly squeezed lemon juice

½ teaspoon sea salt

For the soup

1 tablespoon extra-virgin olive oil

1 yellow onion, diced

1 tablespoon curry powder

2 garlic cloves, minced

1 cup dried green lentils

2 quarts Superfood Vegetable Broth (page 2)

Sea salt

To make the red onion salsa

In a small bowl, stir together the red onion, cilantro, lemon juice, and salt. Set aside.

To make the soup

1. In a large pot over medium heat, heat the olive oil. Add the onion and cook for 5 minutes, until it begins to soften.

2. Stir in the curry powder and garlic and cook for about 1 minute until fragrant.

3. Add the lentils and vegetable broth and bring the soup to a simmer. Taste and season with salt. Partially cover the pot and cook for 20 minutes, or until the lentils are soft.

4. Divide the soup among serving bowls and top with a generous spoonful of salsa.

5. Refrigerate cooled leftovers separately in airtight containers. The salsa will keep for 1 day; the soup for up to 3 days.

PREP TIP The salsa can be prepared up to 2 hours ahead of time. If you wish to make it sooner, keep the lemon juice and salt separate from the onion and cilantro until 2 hours before you intend to serve it.

Per Serving: Total calories: 239; Total fat: 5g; Saturated fat: 1g; Carbohydrates: 37g; Sodium: 620mg; Fiber: 17g; Protein: 16g

SWEET POTATO TORTILLA SOUP

Dairy-Free
Vegan
Serves: 4
Prep time: 10 minutes
Cook time: 25 minutes

The tortilla soup I enjoyed growing up was little more than ground beef, broth, shredded cheese, and loads of tortilla chips—not exactly a superfood soup. Nevertheless, I wanted to capture the fun of the original while packing in lots of nutritional goodness from plants. This soup offers sweet potatoes, black beans, fresh corn, and cilantro along with a generous dose of cumin and smoked paprika. Improve the nutritional value of all the veggies here by adding a few slices of creamy avocado.

2 tablespoons canola oil

1 yellow onion, diced

4 garlic cloves, minced

1 tablespoon ground cumin

1 tablespoon smoked paprika

1 teaspoon ground coriander

1 (15-ounce) can fire-roasted tomatoes with their juices

1 quart Superfood Vegetable Broth (page 2)

2 large sweet potatoes, peeled and diced

1 (15-ounce) can black beans, rinsed and drained

1 cup frozen corn kernels, thawed

½ cup minced fresh cilantro

Juice of 2 or 3 limes

Tortilla chips, for serving

Avocado slices, for serving

1. In a large pot over medium heat, heat the canola oil. Add the onion and cook for 5 minutes, until it begins to soften.

2. Stir in the garlic, cumin, paprika, and coriander. Cook for 1 minute until fragrant.

3. Add the tomatoes, vegetable broth, and sweet potatoes. Bring the soup to a simmer, partially cover the pot, and cook for 10 to 12 minutes, or until the sweet potato is soft.

4. Stir in the black beans and corn and simmer for 1 minute more, just until heated through.

5. Stir in the cilantro and lime juice.

6. Divide the soup among serving bowls and top with tortilla chips and avocado. Or cover and refrigerate for up to 3 days.

SUBSTITUTE IT! Chickpeas also work well in place of the black beans and can mimic the texture of ground meat. Add them to the pot along with the garlic and spices in step 2, mashing them with the back of a fork until they're somewhat broken up.

Per Serving: Total calories: 352; Total fat: 8g; Saturated fat: 1g; Carbohydrates: 59g; Sodium: 440mg; Fiber: 13g; Protein: 13g

RIBOLITTA

Dairy-Free

Vegan

Serves: 4

Prep time:
15 minutes

Cook time:
25 minutes

Extra-virgin olive oil offers more than comforting richness in this soup. It may also provide neuroprotective and cardioprotective benefits, and researchers credit the polyphenols in olive oil for the beneficial effects of a Mediterranean diet. They also point to vegetables, beans, dark leafy greens, and tomatoes as the source of the diet's health benefits, and this soup packs them all in. In keeping with the theme, serve with a robust Italian red wine.

½ cup plus
2 tablespoons
extra-virgin olive
oil, divided

1 yellow onion, diced

4 garlic
cloves, minced

¼ teaspoon red
pepper flakes

½ cup minced
fresh parsley

2 tablespoons
minced fresh
rosemary leaves

1 tablespoon minced
fresh thyme leaves

1 (15-ounce) can
whole plum
tomatoes,
hand crushed

2 quarts Superfood
Vegetable Broth
(page 2), plus
more as needed

1 bunch Swiss chard,
stems diced, leaves
thinly sliced

2 cups hand-torn
stale bread,
crusts removed
(gluten-free,
if needed)

1 (15-ounce) can
cannellini beans,
rinsed and drained

Sea salt

1. In a large pot over medium heat, heat 2 tablespoons of the olive oil. Add the onion and cook for about 7 minutes until mostly soft. Add the garlic and red pepper flakes and cook for 2 minutes more.

2. Stir in the parsley, rosemary, thyme, tomatoes, vegetable broth, and Swiss chard stems. Bring the soup to a simmer and cook for 5 minutes.

3. Add the Swiss chard leaves and cook for 2 minutes more.

4. Stir in the bread and ¼ cup of olive oil. Simmer for 10 to 12 minutes, stirring frequently, until the bread is fully integrated into the soup.

5. Stir in the beans and remaining ¼ cup of olive oil. Taste and season with salt. Cook for 3 to 4 minutes more, until the beans are just heated through. Divide the soup among serving bowls, or cover and refrigerate for up to 3 days. You may wish to thin the leftovers with additional broth.

PREP TIP To make this soup in a slow cooker, complete step 1 on the stove-top. Transfer the onion and garlic to a slow cooker and add all the remaining ingredients. Cover and cook on low heat for 6 hours, or until the bread is fully integrated into the soup.

Per Serving: Total calories: 528; Total fat: 35g; Saturated fat: 5g; Carbohydrates: 45g; Sodium: 767mg; Fiber: 13g; Protein: 14g

ROASTED TOFU
IN SHIITAKE DASHI

Dairy-Free
Vegan
Serves: 4
Prep time:
15 minutes
Cook time:
15 to 20 minutes

Minimally processed soy foods, such as tofu and tempeh, may reduce the risk of coronary heart disease and cancer, alleviate hot flashes and depression, and improve skin health. That's a pretty impressive list of benefits from one of the most pedestrian sources of plant-based protein. The trick to loving this vegetarian standard is learning how to prepare it. I wasted many years trying to pan-sear tofu. It almost always stuck to the pan and I lost the crispy, golden sear I was looking for. Roasting it in the oven was a game changer for me. There's no mess, minimal oil, and a delicious golden-brown crust every time. Give it a try to change your relationship with tofu.

2 tablespoons canola oil

8 ounces fresh mushrooms

1 tablespoon low-sodium soy sauce (gluten-free, if needed)

1 tablespoon cornstarch

1 tablespoon toasted sesame oil

1 (14-ounce) block tofu, drained, pressed, and cut into triangles

2 quarts Kombu Dashi (page 8), made with dried shiitake mushrooms

4 heads baby bok choy, thinly sliced

1 bunch broccolini, trimmed

2 carrots, thinly sliced

1-inch piece fresh ginger, halved lengthwise

2 scallions, thinly sliced on the bias

1. Preheat the oven to 400°F. Line a baking sheet with parchment paper.

2. Heat a large sauté pan or skillet over medium-high heat. When hot, pour in the canola oil and mushrooms. Sear the mushrooms for about

2 minutes on each side until gently browned. You will likely have to do this in batches so as not to crowd the pan. Set aside.

3. In a small bowl, whisk the soy sauce, cornstarch, and sesame oil. Place the tofu into this mixture and gently toss to coat, trying not to break up the tofu. Spread the tofu on the prepared baking sheet and bake for 8 to 10 minutes until gently browned on the bottom. Flip the tofu pieces and bake for 5 minutes more, or until the tofu is crisp and browned.

4. While the tofu cooks, in a large pot over medium heat, bring the dashi to a simmer. Add the bok choy, broccolini, carrots, and ginger. Cook for 3 minutes, until the vegetables are tender and brightly colored. Remove and discard the ginger. Stir in the mushrooms.

5. Divide the soup among serving bowls and top with the roasted tofu pieces and scallions. Or, cover and refrigerate the soup and tofu separately for up to 3 days.

PREP TIP To press tofu, slice the block in half horizontally. Place the pieces side by side on a cutting board, with space between them. Top with a second cutting board and place a cast iron skillet or something else heavy on top of the board. Set this near a sink or over a kitchen cloth to catch the juices. Let sit for at least 15 minutes. You may wish to press down with your hands on the top cutting board or tilt it to allow the juices to run out the sides.

Per Serving: Total calories: 246; Total fat: 16g; Saturated fat: 2g; Carbohydrates: 15g; Sodium: 328mg; Fiber: 4g; Protein: 15g

PERUVIAN QUINOA SOUP WITH CHICKEN AND SALSA VERDE

Dairy-Free
Gluten-Free
Serves: 4
Prep time:
15 minutes
Cook time:
30 minutes

This hearty soup combines two of my favorite Peruvian superfoods—quinoa and sweet potato. Quinoa gets due credit for providing a balance of essential amino acids. It also offers a host of phytochemicals with antioxidant and anti-inflammatory properties. Fresh cilantro, garlic, and jalapeño make a punchy sauce that brings just the right amount of bright acidity and spice to make this soup downright addictive. To make the soup vegan, use the Superfood Vegetable Broth, omit the chicken, and increase the quinoa to 1 cup.

For the soup

1 tablespoon
extra-virgin
olive oil

1 yellow onion,
thinly sliced

2 garlic
cloves, smashed

1 teaspoon
smoked paprika

1 teaspoon
ground cumin

2 quarts Chicken
Broth (page 11)

¾ cup quinoa,
rinsed well

1 cup diced peeled
sweet potato

2 cups shredded
cooked chicken

2 cups fresh
baby spinach

½ cup fresh or frozen
corn kernels

For the salsa verde

1 cup packed
fresh cilantro

1 jalapeño pepper,
cored and diced

1 large garlic
clove, peeled

Juice of 1 lime

¼ cup extra-virgin
olive oil

Sea salt

To make the soup

1. In a large pot over medium heat, heat the olive oil. Add the onion and cook for 10 minutes, until very soft. Add the garlic, paprika, and cumin. Cook for 1 minute, just until fragrant.

2. Add the chicken broth and bring the soup to a simmer.

3. Stir in the quinoa and sweet potato. Cover the pot and cook for 12 to 14 minutes, just until the quinoa is soft.

4. Stir in the chicken, spinach, and corn. Set aside.

To make the salsa verde

1. In a food processor, combine the cilantro, jalapeño, and garlic. Pulse until finely chopped.

2. Stir in the lime juice and olive oil. Taste and season with salt.

3. Divide the soup among serving dishes and top with the salsa verde. Or, chill and refrigerate the soup and salsa verde in separate airtight containers for up to 2 days.

TASTE TIP Avoid blending extra-virgin olive oil. The blades disturb the molecular composition of the oil and release bitter compounds. That's okay when oil is used in a small quantity or with other strong flavors that will mask that bitterness, but it's noticeable in recipes like this one.

Per Serving: Total calories: 545; Total fat: 27g; Saturated fat: 4g; Carbohydrates: 46g; Sodium: 393mg; Fiber: 8g; Protein: 31g

THAI COCONUT CURRY SOUP WITH CHICKEN

Dairy-Free
Gluten-Free
Serves: 4
Prep time:
15 minutes
Cook time:
15 minutes

Red curry is one of my favorite dishes to order in Thai restaurants. I love its creaminess and fragrant aroma. Although most of the fat in coconut is saturated, epidemiological studies—studies of populations—have found that in groups where a significant percentage of calories come from coconut, cardiovascular disease is virtually nonexistent. The red curry paste infuses the coconut milk with flavor. This recipe includes the traditional Thai vegetables—green beans, mushrooms, and tomatoes—but you can use whatever vegetables you have on hand.

- 1 tablespoon coconut oil or extra-virgin olive oil
- 1 yellow onion, halved and thinly sliced
- 2 garlic cloves, minced
- 2 tablespoons red curry paste
- 1 tablespoon coconut sugar, or light brown sugar
- 1 tablespoon fish sauce
- 1 (14-ounce) can full-fat coconut milk
- 2 quarts Chicken Broth (page 11)
- 4 ounces thin green beans, trimmed and cut into 2-inch pieces
- 4 ounces cremini mushrooms, halved
- 2 plum tomatoes, quartered
- 2 tablespoons freshly squeezed lime juice
- 2 cups shredded cooked chicken (from the Chicken Broth recipe)
- Handful fresh cilantro, roughly chopped

1. In a large pot over medium-high heat, heat the coconut oil. Add the onion and sauté for 5 minutes, until gently browned on the edges.

2. Stir in the garlic, curry paste, and coconut sugar. Cook for about 1 minute, until fragrant. Add the fish sauce, coconut milk, and chicken broth. Bring the soup to a simmer.

3. Add the green beans and mushrooms and cook for 2 minutes.

4. Add the tomatoes and cook for 1 minute more. Stir in the lime juice and chicken, simmering the soup for 3 to 4 minutes, until the chicken is just warmed through.

5. Divide the soup among serving dishes and top with the cilantro. Or cover and refrigerate for up to 2 days.

SUBSTITUTE IT! To make this soup plant-based, swap the fish sauce for gluten-free soy sauce and use Superfood Vegetable Broth (page 2) with 2 cups of cooked chickpeas in place of the chicken broth and chicken, respectively.

Per Serving: Total calories: 467; Total fat: 31g; Saturated fat: 20g; Carbohydrates: 19g; Sodium: 1,129mg; Fiber: 4g; Protein: 27g

CHARD AND POTATO SOUP

Dairy-Free
Easy Prep
Gluten-Free
Vegan
Serves: 4
Prep time:
10 minutes
Cook time:
15 minutes

This hearty winter soup combines Swiss chard and Yukon Gold potatoes in an earthy mushroom broth with rosemary and thyme. Dark leafy green vegetables, such as chard, are an excellent source of potassium, which can help reduce the risk of stroke. Calorie for calorie, the vegetable has five times as much potassium as a banana. This soup gets better as it sits, so make it a day ahead and enjoy after a long day of hiking or skiing.

2 tablespoons
  extra-virgin
  olive oil

1 yellow onion,
  thinly sliced

4 garlic
  cloves, smashed

1 (15-ounce) can
  whole plum
  tomatoes,
  hand-torn

1 pound Yukon Gold
  potatoes, cut into
  1-inch pieces

2 thyme sprigs

1 rosemary sprig

2 quarts Mushroom
  Broth (page 6)

1 bunch Swiss chard,
  stems diced, leaves
  thinly sliced

Sea salt

1. In a large pot over medium heat, heat the olive oil. Add the onion and garlic. Cook for 5 minutes, until they begin to soften.

2. Stir in the tomatoes, potatoes, thyme, rosemary, and mushroom broth. Bring the soup to a simmer. Cook for 5 minutes.

3. Add the Swiss chard and cook for 5 minutes more. Taste and season with salt. Remove and discard the rosemary and thyme sprigs.

4. Serve immediately or cover and refrigerate for up to 3 days.

SUBSTITUTE IT! Use another small waxy potato in place of the Yukon Golds, if you wish.

Per Serving: Total calories: 242; Total fat: 9g; Saturated fat: 1g; Carbohydrates: 37g; Sodium: 399mg; Fiber: 9g; Protein: 8g

VEGAN CORN CHOWDER

Dairy-Free
Easy Prep
Gluten-Free
Vegan
Serves: 4
Prep time:
15 minutes
Cook time:
25 minutes

Have you ever heard of corn milk? It's not commercially available, and you won't find it next to the almond milk, soy milk, or other plant-based milk alternatives. It's at its best when made from fresh corn. Not only does it bring a summery flavor to this soup, its starches naturally thicken the soup as well. No heavy cream needed.

8 ears corn, kernels cut from the cobs, divided

2 tablespoons extra-virgin olive oil

1 small leek, washed well and finely chopped

1 small onion, diced

1 celery stalk, minced

1 small carrot, minced

Sea salt

¼ cup dry white wine

2 quarts Superfood Vegetable Broth (page 2)

1 tablespoon Old Bay Seasoning

2 tarragon sprigs, leaves only, minced

1. Begin by making the corn milk. Run half the corn kernels through a juicer. If you don't have a juicer, put them in a blender and puree until smooth. Strain through a fine-mesh sieve or a nut milk bag set over a bowl.

2. In a large pot over medium heat, heat the olive oil. Add the leek, onion, celery, and carrot. Season with salt and cook for 15 minutes, until very soft. Do not brown.

3. Add the white wine and cook for 2 minutes, or until most of the liquid is evaporated.

4. Add the vegetable broth, Old Bay, and corn milk. Bring to a simmer and cook for 5 minutes.

5. Using an immersion blender, puree the soup until smooth.

Continued ▶

6. Stir in the remaining corn kernels and tarragon and cook for 2 minutes, just until the corn is heated through.

7. Refrigerate cooled leftovers in an airtight container for up to 3 days.

TASTE TIP For even more creaminess, add ¼ cup of sour cream or vegan sour cream in step 4.

Per Serving: Total calories: 282; Total fat: 9g; Saturated fat: 1g; Carbohydrates: 47g; Sodium: 1,296mg; Fiber: 9g; Protein: 9g

ROASTED SQUASH, BEANS, AND CORN

Dairy-Free
Easy Prep
Gluten-Free
Vegan
Serves: 4
Prep time:
10 minutes
Cook time:
1 hour, 30 minutes

Squash, beans, and corn are considered the "three sisters." Indigenous people in the Americas planted the seeds close together, providing advantages to the growing plants. They're equally beneficial together in a plant-based meal, providing all the essential amino acids in one dish. Serve with warmed tortillas and plenty of fresh pico de gallo.

1½ cups dried pinto beans, soaked in water overnight, drained

2 quarts Superfood Vegetable Broth (page 2)

4 cups diced calabaza squash, or butternut squash

2 tablespoons canola oil

Sea salt

1 yellow onion, diced

6 garlic cloves, minced

2 teaspoons dried oregano

1 cup fresh or frozen corn kernels

1. Preheat the oven to 400°F.

2. In a large pot over high heat, combine the pinto beans and vegetable broth. Bring the broth to a simmer. Partially cover the pot and reduce the heat to maintain a simmer. Cook for 1 hour, until the beans are nearly soft.

3. While the beans cook, on a large rimmed sheet pan, toss together the squash and canola oil to coat the squash. Spread it into a single layer and season with salt.

4. Roast for about 30 minutes, until browned and tender. Remove and set aside.

5. When the beans are nearly soft, add the onion, garlic, and oregano to the pot. Cook for 30 minutes, or until the vegetables are very soft. Taste and season with salt.

Continued ▶

6. Stir in the roasted squash and corn and cook for 3 to 4 minutes, just until heated through.

7. Refrigerate cooled leftovers in an airtight container for up to 3 days.

POWER UP! To reduce gas associated with beans, add one piece of kombu in step 2. Remove it in step 5 before adding the onion, garlic, and oregano. Kombu contains enzymes that help break down the sugars in beans to make them more digestible.

Per Serving: Total calories: 402; Total fat: 8g; Saturated fat: 1g; Carbohydrates: 72g; Sodium: 325mg; Fiber: 17g; Protein: 16g

TOMATO-LIME SOUP
WITH CHICKPEAS

Dairy-Free
Gluten-Free
Vegan
Serves: 4
Prep time:
10 minutes
Cook time:
20 minutes

Win over even avowed carnivores with the benefits of this bold soup. Chickpeas, tomatoes, and avocado all contribute prebiotics, which nurture the gut microbiome.

1 tablespoon
  extra-virgin
  olive oil

1 green bell pepper,
  cored and diced

1 red bell pepper,
  cored and diced

1 yellow onion, diced

4 garlic
  cloves, minced

1 tablespoon
  ground cumin

1 tablespoon
  smoked paprika

½ teaspoon
  ground coriander

1 tablespoon white
  wine vinegar

1 pint grape
  tomatoes, halved

2 quarts Superfood
  Vegetable Broth
  (page 2)

2 (15-ounce) cans
  chickpeas, rinsed
  and drained

3 tablespoons freshly
  squeezed lime juice

2 large
  avocados, diced

¼ cup roughly
  chopped
  fresh cilantro

1. In a large pot over medium-high heat, heat the olive oil. Add the green and red bell peppers and onion. Sauté for about 5 minutes, until fragrant and beginning to brown.

2. Stir in the garlic, cumin, paprika, and coriander. Cook for about 30 seconds, until fragrant.

3. Add the vinegar, tomatoes, vegetable broth, and chickpeas. Reduce the heat and simmer the soup for 10 minutes.

Continued ▶

4. Stir in the lime juice, avocados, and cilantro.

5. Refrigerate cooled leftovers in an airtight container for up to 3 days.

SUBSTITUTE IT! If you want something a little meatier, swap the vegetable broth and chickpeas for chicken broth and chicken.

Per Serving: Total calories: 484; Total fat: 21g; Saturated fat: 3g; Carbohydrates: 64g; Sodium: 332mg; Fiber: 23g; Protein: 17g

WILD RICE AND CHORIZO SOUP

Dairy-Free
Gluten-Free
Serves: 4
Prep time:
10 minutes
Cook time:
40 minutes

Wild rice has documented cardiovascular benefits and the ability to reduce cholesterol levels. Plus, it's also packed with antioxidants. A hint of spicy chorizo rounds out the soup: A mere 4 ounces gives the entire soup a generous dose of spice and flavor.

4 ounces chorizo, crumbled (see tip)

1 tablespoon extra-virgin olive oil

2 shallots, halved and thinly sliced

2 garlic cloves, minced

1 tablespoon minced fresh rosemary leaves

1½ cups wild rice

Sea salt

Freshly ground black pepper

2 tablespoons balsamic vinegar

2 quarts Chicken Broth (page 11)

1 cup shredded cooked chicken meat (from the Chicken Broth recipe)

¼ cup roughly chopped fresh parsley

1. In a large pot over medium-high heat, cook the chorizo for 3 to 5 minutes until just cooked through. Using a slotted spoon, transfer the chorizo to a plate.

2. Return the pot to the stove and reduce the heat to medium. Add the olive oil, shallots, garlic, and rosemary. Cook for about 5 minutes, until the vegetables are nearly soft.

3. Stir in the wild rice, stirring until well coated in the oil. Allow the rice to toast for about 1 minute. Generously season with salt and pepper.

4. Add the vinegar to the pot and cook until it is mostly evaporated.

5. Add the chicken broth to the pot and the cooked chorizo. Cover the pot and simmer for 25 minutes, or until the rice is tender.

Continued ▶

6. Stir in the chicken and parsley and cook for 1 or 2 minutes, until the chicken is just heated through. Serve immediately or cover and refrigerate for up to 2 days.

PREP TIP Purchase bulk raw chorizo from a well-stocked meat counter, instead of the cured meat.

Per Serving: Total calories: 544; Total fat: 19g; Saturated fat: 5g; Carbohydrates: 60g; Sodium: 693mg; Fiber: 5g; Protein: 30g

ROASTED KABOCHA SQUASH LAKSA

Dairy-Free
Gluten-Free
Serves: 6
Prep time:
15 minutes
Cook time:
20 minutes

There are as many versions of *laksa* as there are cooks in Southeast Asia. Nevertheless, there probably aren't many made with kabocha squash. This one combines one of my favorite winter squashes with coconut milk and shredded chicken. Kabocha and other winter squashes help stabilize blood sugar and are a rich source of carotenoids, which can be converted into vitamin A.

1 small kabocha squash, seeded and cut into 1-inch pieces

4 tablespoons extra-virgin olive oil, divided

Sea salt

1 small red onion, halved, thinly sliced

1 tablespoon light brown sugar

1 tablespoon minced peeled fresh ginger

2 teaspoons minced garlic

2 tablespoons fish sauce

1 cup full-fat coconut milk

2 quarts Chicken Broth (page 11)

4 ounces brown rice noodles

2 cups shredded cooked chicken (from the Chicken Broth recipe)

3 tablespoons freshly squeezed lime juice

¼ cup roughly chopped fresh mint leaves

¼ cup roughly chopped fresh cilantro

¼ cup roughly chopped peanuts

1. Preheat the oven to 400°F. Line a baking sheet with parchment paper.

2. On the prepared baking sheet, toss the squash with 2 tablespoons of olive oil to coat and season with salt.

3. Roast for 20 minutes, flipping the squash once or twice, until golden brown.

Continued ▶

4. Meanwhile, in a large pot over medium-high heat, heat the remaining 2 tablespoons of olive oil. Add the onion and sauté for 5 minutes, until it begins to brown.

5. Add the brown sugar, ginger, and garlic. Cook for 1 minute until fragrant. Stir in the fish sauce, coconut milk, and chicken broth. Bring the soup to a simmer.

6. Add the rice noodles and cook for 5 minutes, or until nearly softened.

7. Stir in the cooked chicken, roasted squash, and lime juice. Divide the soup among serving dishes and top with the mint, cilantro, and peanuts. Or, cover and refrigerate for up to 2 days.

PREP TIP To prepare the kabocha squash, halve it vertically, scoop out the seeds and strings from each half, then stand each half, cut-side down, on a cutting board. Slice into half-moons. Then slice each half-moon into 1-inch cubes.

Per Serving: Total calories: 427; Total fat: 24g; Saturated fat: 9g; Carbohydrates: 33g; Sodium: 720mg; Fiber: 5g; Protein: 20g

FARRO AND WILD MUSHROOM SOUP

Dairy-Free
Vegan
Serves: 4
Prep time: 15 minutes
Cook time: 45 minutes

Earthy wild mushrooms and nutty farro make this soup hearty, flavorful, and filling. Research published by Johns Hopkins University suggests swapping mushrooms for meat for one meal a day can help you lose weight, reduce overall body fat, and maintain a leaner body over time.

¼ cup extra-virgin olive oil

1 yellow onion, minced

4 garlic cloves, minced

2 thyme sprigs, leaves only

1 tablespoon minced fresh rosemary leaves

8 ounces assorted mushrooms, such as shiitake, oyster, and maitake, roughly chopped

1 cup farro

Sea salt

Freshly ground black pepper

½ cup dry white wine

2 quarts Mushroom Broth (page 6)

1 (15-ounce) can chickpeas, rinsed and drained

1. In a large pot over medium heat, heat the olive oil. Add the onion and cook for 5 minutes, until it begins to soften. Add the garlic, thyme, rosemary, and mushrooms. Cook for 2 minutes.

2. Stir in the farro, stirring until well coated in the oil. Toast it in the pot for 2 minutes. Generously season with salt and pepper.

3. Add the white wine and simmer until most of the liquid is absorbed, stirring frequently.

Continued ▶

4. Add the mushroom broth and return the soup to a simmer. Cover the pot and cook for 30 minutes, or until the farro is tender.

5. Stir in the chickpeas and cook for 2 minutes. Serve immediately or cover and refrigerate for up to 3 days.

SUBSTITUTE IT! To make this gluten-free, use wild rice or millet in place of the farro.

Per Serving: Total calories: 506; Total fat: 18g; Saturated fat: 2g; Carbohydrates: 72g; Sodium: 15mg; Fiber: 14g; Protein: 16g

WHITE BEAN CIOPPINO

Dairy-Free
Gluten-Free
Vegan
Serves: 4
Prep time:
10 minutes
Cook time:
30 minutes

As much as I love traditional cioppino with fresh fish and shellfish, it's challenging to find sustainably sourced seafood that isn't contaminated with oceanic pollutants, such as mercury and microplastics. Hence, I find myself eating less and less seafood. Nevertheless, I love the flavors of this traditional Italian stew. I replaced the seafood with beans—not only are they healthier, they're also much less expensive. The Kombu Dashi gives the soup a hint of the sea and may improve the digestibility of the beans.

¼ cup extra-virgin olive oil

6 garlic cloves, minced

2 shallots, thinly sliced

Pinch red pepper flakes

1 (28-ounce) can whole plum tomatoes, hand crushed, juices reserved for another use

1 tablespoon minced fresh thyme leaves

2 tablespoons harissa, plus more for serving

½ cup dry white wine

2 quarts Kombu Dashi (page 8)

2 (14-ounce) cans cannellini beans, rinsed and drained

½ cup minced fresh parsley

2 scallions, thinly sliced, white and green parts

Juice of ½ lemon

Sea salt

Freshly ground pepper

1. In a large pot over medium heat, heat the olive oil. Add the garlic, shallots, and red pepper flakes. Cook for 5 minutes, until somewhat soft.

2. Add the tomatoes and thyme. Cook for 15 minutes until the tomatoes are pulpy and begin to lose some of the liquid. Reduce the heat if they begin sticking to the pan.

3. Stir in the harissa and cook for 1 minute until fragrant.

4. Add the white wine and cook for about 2 minutes to evaporate some of the alcohol.

Continued ▶

5. Stir in the dashi, beans, and parsley. Simmer, uncovered, for 5 minutes.

6. Stir in the scallions and lemon juice. Taste and season with salt and pepper.

7. Refrigerate any leftovers in an airtight container for up to 3 days.

TASTE TIP Harissa is a North African chili paste with caraway and cumin. They're unlikely spices in cioppino, but bring a welcome complexity to the soup. You can find harissa in well-stocked grocery stores or online.

Per Serving: Total calories: 408; Total fat: 15g; Saturated fat: 2g; Carbohydrates: 51g; Sodium: 426mg; Fiber: 13g; Protein: 16g

RED LENTIL DAL

Dairy-Free
Easy Prep
Gluten-Free
Vegan
Serves: 4
Prep time:
15 minutes
Cook time:
30 minutes

With a monochromatic golden red hue, this soup has an unassuming vibe. But it's loaded with flavor and nutrition. A 2017 review of the scientific literature found that polyphenol-rich lentils possess antioxidant and anti-inflammatory properties and may reduce the risk of diabetes, obesity, high cholesterol, and cancer. That's high praise for such a humble legume. Serve this with garlic naan bread and a drizzle of yogurt.

2 tablespoons
canola oil

1 yellow onion, diced

1 carrot, minced

Sea salt

4 large garlic
cloves, minced

1 tablespoon minced
peeled fresh ginger

1 tablespoon
curry powder

1 teaspoon
ground cumin

Pinch red
pepper flakes

1 cup dried red lentils

1 quart Superfood
Vegetable Broth
(page 2)

1 (14-ounce)
can full-fat
coconut milk

2 tablespoons
tomato paste

Juice of 1 lime

1. In a large pot over medium heat, heat the canola oil. Add the onion and carrot, generously season with salt, and cook for 5 minutes, until the vegetables begin to soften. Add the garlic and ginger and cook for 1 to 2 minutes, until fragrant.

2. Stir in the curry powder, cumin, and red pepper flakes. Toast the spices for about 1 minute.

3. Stir in the lentils, vegetable broth, coconut milk, and tomato paste. Bring the soup to a simmer. Cover the pot and cook on low heat for about 15 minutes, or until the lentils are tender.

4. Stir in the lime juice. Taste and season with more salt, as needed. Serve immediately or cover and refrigerate for up to 3 days.

Continued ▶

Red Lentil Dal, *continued*

POWER UP! Improve the cancer-fighting power of this soup by adding more turmeric (there's some in the curry powder) and topping the soup with quick pickled red onions. Together, the two are even more potent—a phenomenon known as food synergy (see page 66). Cut half a red onion into very thin slices and cover with lime juice and a pinch of sea salt.

Per Serving: Total calories: 447; Total fat: 25g; Saturated fat: 16g; Carbohydrates: 41g; Sodium: 430mg; Fiber: 11g; Protein: 16g

CAULIFLOWER CURRY

Dairy-Free
Gluten-Free
Vegan
Serves: 4
Prep time:
15 minutes
Cook time:
30 minutes

Vibrant yellow turmeric brightens up cauliflower in this vegan stew. The active ingredient in turmeric, curcumin, boasts many health benefits, and new research indicates it's also excellent for healthy skin and has shown results in treating a variety of dermatologic conditions.

2 tablespoons extra-virgin olive oil

1 yellow onion, minced

5 garlic cloves, minced

2 tablespoons curry powder

2 tablespoons tomato paste

2 Yukon Gold potatoes, cut into 2-inch chunks

1 head cauliflower, broken into florets

½ cup dried yellow lentils, or yellow split peas

1 cup full-fat coconut milk

1 quart Superfood Vegetable Broth (page 2)

¼ cup golden raisins

½ cup slivered almonds, toasted

Sea salt

Freshly ground black pepper

1 tablespoon freshly squeezed lime juice

¼ cup minced fresh cilantro

Cooked basmati rice, for serving

1. In a large pot over medium-high heat, heat the olive oil. Add the onion and cook for 5 minutes, until it begins to soften. Add the garlic and curry powder and cook for 1 minute more. Stir in the tomato paste and cook for 30 seconds.

2. Add the potatoes, cauliflower, lentils, coconut milk, vegetable broth, raisins, and almonds. Generously season the soup with salt and pepper. Cover the pot and cook on medium-low heat for 20 minutes, or until the lentils and vegetables are tender.

3. Stir in the lime juice and fresh cilantro. Serve over basmati rice.

Continued ▶

Cauliflower Curry, *continued*

SIMPLIFY IT! The dish can also be made in a slow cooker. In a slow cooker, combine all the ingredients, stir, cover, and cook on low heat for 6 hours, or on high heat for 2½ hours.

Per Serving: Total calories: 456; Total fat: 22g; Saturated fat: 10g; Carbohydrates: 55g; Sodium: 449mg; Fiber: 13g; Protein: 16g

WHITE BEAN AND KALE SOUP

Dairy-Free
Easy Prep
Gluten-Free
Serves: 4
Prep time:
10 minutes
Cook time:
40 minutes

Maca and acai rise and fall in popularity, but kale remains the superfood that never loses its luster. Kale is listed on the Centers for Disease Control's list of 41 powerhouse fruits and vegetables, ranking right in the middle of the list for nutrient density.

2 tablespoons
    extra-virgin olive oil

1 leek, cleaned well
    and thinly sliced

1 yellow onion, diced

½ celery stalk, diced

Sea salt

4 garlic cloves, minced

1 tablespoon minced
    fresh thyme leaves

Pinch red
    pepper flakes

1 bunch kale, stems
    finely chopped,
    leaves thinly sliced

2 quarts Superfood
    Vegetable Broth
    (page 2)

1 (15-ounce) can white
    beans, drained
    but not rinsed

Freshly ground
    black pepper

1. In a large pot over medium heat, heat the olive oil. Add the leek, onion, celery, and a generous pinch of salt. Cook for 12 to 15 minutes, or until the vegetables are very tender.

2. Add the garlic, thyme, and red pepper flakes. Cook for 1 minute.

3. Stir in the kale stems and vegetable broth. Bring the soup to a simmer and cook for 5 minutes.

4. Add the kale leaves and white beans. Season with pepper. Simmer the soup for 20 minutes, until the kale is very soft. Divide the soup among serving bowls, or cover and refrigerate for up to 3 days.

TASTE TIP To really amp up the flavor in this soup, add a Parmesan rind in step 2. Remove it before serving.

Per Serving: Total calories: 233; Total fat: 8g; Saturated fat: 1g; Carbohydrates: 34g; Sodium: 345mg; Fiber: 10g; Protein: 11g

Wild Salmon and Soba Hot Pot, page 109

CHAPTER FIVE

Noodle Soups

What is pasta doing in a superfood cookbook? Bringing a host of nutritional benefits from healthy whole grains, that's what! They're excellent sources of prebiotics, phytonutrients, phytates, and antioxidants. And whole grains have been shown to improve vascular health, nurture the gut microbiome, improve bone density, and even fight cancer, among many other documented benefits.

This chapter explores soups from many noodle-loving cultures—from a clean, simple Japanese Vegetable Soba (page 100) to a hearty Italian Kale and Orzo Minestrone with Pistou (page 111). It also swaps the carb-rich pasta for equally healthy vegetable noodles in Ginger Chicken Zoodle Soup (page 107) and Sweet Miso and Carrot Noodle Soup (page 113).

VEGETABLE SOBA

Dairy-Free
Gluten-Free
Vegan
Serves: 4
Prep time:
10 minutes
Cook time:
15 minutes

Soba's distinct nutty flavor is from buckwheat, a gluten-free grain with a long list of health benefits. It has been shown to reduce cholesterol levels, protect against brain aging, fight cancer, reduce inflammation, and counteract diabetes and hypertension. If that weren't enough, it's also a potent prebiotic, which helps nurture a healthy gut microbiome. In this recipe it's paired with blanched dandelion greens, peppery watermelon radishes, and scallions. If you can find enoki mushrooms, add a handful to the soup along with the other vegetables. They're an excellent source of antioxidants.

1 bunch dandelion greens

8 ounces soba noodles (choose 100-percent buckwheat noodles for gluten-free)

2 quarts Kombu Dashi (page 8)

4 watermelon radishes, trimmed and thinly sliced

4 ounces enoki mushrooms, or thinly sliced cremini mushrooms

2 scallions, thinly sliced

1 tablespoon toasted sesame oil

Togarashi, or red pepper flakes, for seasoning

1. Bring a large pot of salted water to a boil over high heat. Add the dandelion greens and cook for about 1 minute until bright green. Use a spider or a fine-mesh strainer to transfer the greens to a colander and rinse with cool running water.

2. Return the water in the pot to a boil and cook the soba noodles according to the package directions. Drain. Divide the soba noodles and dandelion greens among serving bowls.

3. Meanwhile, in a saucepan over low heat, bring the dashi to the barest simmer. Divide it among serving bowls and top the soup with the radishes, mushrooms, and scallions. Drizzle toasted sesame oil over each bowl and season with togarashi.

4. Refrigerate cooled leftovers in an airtight container for up to 3 days.

TASTE TIP Togarashi is a Japanese chili powder with toasted seaweed, orange peel, and sesame seeds. It adds spice and a bit of umami to any dish. Use it as you would freshly ground black pepper.

Per Serving: Total calories: 255; Total fat: 5g; Saturated fat: 1g; Carbohydrates: 45g; Sodium: 242mg; Fiber: 3g; Protein: 11g

GREEN CURRY SHRIMP NOODLE SOUP

Dairy-Free
Gluten-Free
Serves: 4
Prep time:
10 minutes
Cook time:
15 minutes

Sweet, spicy, tangy green curry serves as a delicious backdrop for whatever healthy vegetables are in season. Coconut milk contains phenolic compounds and cytokinins that may assist in preventing Alzheimer's disease. I prefer to use full-fat coconut milk because you can always water it down if you wish. Why buy it with added water and thickeners? Mirin is a Japanese sweet rice wine. Mirin and orange juice bring a pleasant balance of sweetness and acidity to the dish. If you can't find mirin or don't care to buy it, use white wine. If you want to skip the wine altogether, substitute 1 tablespoon white wine vinegar or rice vinegar.

- 2 tablespoons canola oil
- 4 large garlic cloves, minced
- 1 tablespoon minced peeled fresh ginger
- 1 small onion, halved and thinly sliced
- 1 lemongrass stalk, bottom 3 inches removed and halved, remaining 12 inches or so discarded

- ¼ cup Thai green curry paste
- ¼ cup mirin
- ¼ cup freshly squeezed orange juice
- 2 quarts Fish Stock (page 10)
- 1 (15-ounce) can full-fat coconut milk
- 8 ounces green beans, trimmed and cut into 2-inch pieces

- 1 pound jumbo shrimp, peeled and deveined
- 8 ounces brown rice noodles, soaked in water (see tip)
- 1 cup roughly chopped fresh Thai basil, or Italian basil
- 2 limes, cut into wedges

1. In a large pot over medium heat, heat the canola oil. Add the garlic, ginger, onion, and lemongrass. Cook for about 5 minutes, until the vegetables begin to soften, being careful not to burn the garlic.

2. Stir in the curry paste, mirin, and orange juice. Simmer the mixture for 2 to 3 minutes, until some of the liquid has evaporated.

3. Add the fish stock and coconut milk and bring the soup to a simmer.

4. Add the green beans and shrimp. Cook for about 3 minutes, or until the shrimp are cooked through (pink and opaque) and the green beans are bright green. Remove and discard the lemongrass pieces.

5. Drain and divide the rice noodles among serving bowls. Ladle the curry over each bowl and garnish with basil and lime wedges.

6. Refrigerate leftovers in an airtight container for up to 2 days.

PREP TIP To soak the brown rice noodles, bring a large pot of salted water to a boil. Add the noodles. Remove the pan from the heat and let soak for 10 minutes, or until completely soft. Drain.

Per Serving: Total calories: 685; Total fat: 28g; Saturated fat: 16g; Carbohydrates: 68g; Sodium: 773mg; Fiber: 7g; Protein: 35g

VEGAN MINESTRONE

Dairy-Free
Easy Prep
Vegan
Serves: 4
Prep time:
10 minutes
Cook time:
40 minutes

This hearty minestrone is loaded with garlic, a superfood that's as pungent as it is potent. Researchers from Qatar found that garlic has the potential to treat mild hypertension, to decrease hypercholesterolemia, and prevent atherosclerosis. While they recommend more research to figure out exactly why, it's reason enough to add a few extra cloves to this soup.

- ¼ cup extra-virgin olive oil
- 6 garlic cloves, minced
- 2 celery stalks, diced
- 2 carrots, diced
- 1 onion, diced
- Sea salt
- ¼ cup minced fresh parsley
- 2 tablespoons minced fresh thyme leaves
- 1 (28-ounce) can whole plum tomatoes, drained
- ¼ cup dry red wine
- 2 quarts Superfood Vegetable Broth (page 2) or Chicken Broth (page 11, for a non-vegan/vegetarian soup)
- 8 ounces whole-grain pasta, such as elbow macaroni or shells
- 8 ounces green beans, trimmed
- 1 (15-ounce) can kidney beans, rinsed and drained
- 1 cup roughly chopped fresh basil
- Freshly ground black pepper

1. In a large pot over medium heat, heat the olive oil. Add the garlic, celery, carrots, onion, and a generous pinch of salt. Cook for about 10 minutes, or until soft. Stir the parsley and thyme.

2. Hand crush the tomatoes and add them to the pot. Simmer the soup for about 10 minutes, until much of the liquid has evaporated.

3. Add the red wine and cook for 2 minutes.

4. Add the vegetable broth and bring the soup to a simmer.

5. Add the pasta and cook for 5 minutes. Add the green beans and cook for 5 minutes more, or until the pasta is tender.

6. Stir in the kidney beans and simmer for 2 to 3 minutes, until just warmed through.

7. Stir in the basil. Serve immediately or cover and refrigerate the soup for up to 4 days. Season with black pepper.

SUBSTITUTE IT! You don't have to use all the olive oil in this recipe. It does provide a rich body to the soup, but if you're limiting fat intake, reduce it to as little as 2 teaspoons. Keep a close eye on the vegetables in step 1 to make sure they don't burn.

Per Serving: Total calories: 522; Total fat: 14g; Saturated fat: 2g; Carbohydrates: 83g; Sodium: 604mg; Fiber: 18g; Protein: 18g

IMMUNE-BOOSTING CHICKEN NOODLE SOUP

Dairy-Free
Easy Prep
Serves: 4
Prep time:
10 minutes
Cook time:
25 minutes

Garlic and chicken broth have clinically proven benefits in boosting your immune system. But what if you've already come down with something? Not to worry—chicken broth has been shown to loosen up chest congestion.

2 tablespoons olive oil

8 garlic cloves, minced

2 carrots, minced

2 celery stalks, minced

Sea salt

1 tablespoon minced fresh thyme leaves

2 quarts Chicken Broth (page 11)

4 cups shredded cooked chicken (from the Chicken Broth recipe)

8 ounces whole-grain spaghetti, broken into pieces

Freshly ground black pepper

2 tablespoons minced fresh parsley

1. In a large pot over medium-high heat, heat the olive oil. Add the garlic, carrots, celery, and a generous pinch of salt. Cook for 5 minutes. Add the thyme.

2. Pour in the chicken broth and chicken, and bring the soup to a simmer. Cook for 5 minutes.

3. Add the pasta and simmer for 7 to 9 minutes, until tender. Taste and season with salt and pepper. Serve immediately, or cover and refrigerate for up to 2 days. Garnish with parsley.

PREP TIP If you prefer larger chunks of vegetables, cut them into ¼-inch slices.

Per Serving: Total calories: 586; Total fat: 20g; Saturated fat: 4g; Carbohydrates: 52g; Sodium: 459mg; Fiber: 9g; Protein: 49g

GINGER CHICKEN ZOODLE SOUP

Dairy-Free
Easy Prep
Gluten-Free
Serves: 4
Prep time:
20 minutes
Cook time:
15 minutes

For a lighter and refreshing take on classic chicken noodle soup, use fresh ginger and tender zucchini noodles. Swapping traditional pasta for vegetables makes the soup naturally gluten-free. Key word: naturally. Many gluten-free foods are filled with highly refined starches, such as potato starch, tapioca starch, and cornstarch. Zucchini noodles are a healthier gluten-free alternative.

2 zucchinis

Sea salt

1 tablespoon
canola oil

1 tablespoon minced
peeled fresh ginger

2 garlic
cloves, minced

1 carrot, sliced

1 celery stalk, minced

2 quarts Chicken
Broth (page 11)

4 cups shredded
cooked chicken
(from Chicken
Broth recipe)

1. Trim the stem end from the zucchinis and halve them widthwise so you have two roughly 4-inch segments. One at a time, fit them onto a spiralizer and run them through the smallest noodle setting. Spread the noodles in a colander and generously season with salt. Place the colander in the sink and let sit for 10 minutes.

2. Meanwhile, in a large pot over medium heat, heat the canola oil. Add the ginger, garlic, carrot, celery, and a pinch of salt. Cook for 5 minutes until the vegetables begin to soften, being careful not to burn the garlic.

3. Add the chicken broth and bring the soup to a simmer. Cook for 5 minutes.

Continued ▶

4. Rinse the zucchini noodles under cool running water and squeeze excess moisture from the noodles with your hands. Add the noodles and chicken to the pot. Simmer for 2 to 3 minutes, until just heated through. Serve immediately, or cover and refrigerate for up to 2 days.

PREP TIP Leaving the zucchini peel on retains more nutrients, but if you prefer an appearance more like traditional pasta, peel the zucchini before running it through the spiralizer.

Per Serving: Total calories: 368; Total fat: 16g; Saturated fat: 4g; Carbohydrates: 10g; Sodium: 438mg; Fiber: 4g; Protein: 44g

WILD SALMON
AND SOBA HOT POT

Dairy-Free
Easy Prep
Gluten-Free
Serves: 4
Prep time:
10 minutes
Cook time:
25 minutes

While the evidence for fish oil remains unconvincing, eating actual fish has pronounced benefits for mood health. A 2016 meta-analysis found that high fish consumption can reduce the risk of depression. Choose wild fish for the most nutrition and the lowest impact environmentally. This tasty soup features wild salmon, healthy buckwheat noodles, and tender spring vegetables in a flavorful kombu dashi.

8 ounces
 soba noodles

2 quarts Kombu
 Dashi (page 8)

¼ cup mirin

2 tablespoons
 gluten-free
 soy sauce

1 carrot, julienned

4 ounces snow
 peas, trimmed

½ bunch tender
 asparagus, tough
 woody ends
 trimmed, remaining
 spears cut into
 2-inch pieces

1 pound wild salmon

1. Bring a large pot of salted water to a boil over high heat. Add the soba noodles and cook according to the package directions, about 8 minutes. Drain and divide the noodles among serving bowls.

2. While the soba noodles cook, in a large pot over medium-low heat, heat the dashi. Add the mirin and soy sauce.

3. Stir in the carrot, snow peas, and asparagus. Add the salmon on top of the vegetables. Cover the pot and gently simmer (at the barest simmer) for 8 minutes, or until the vegetables are tender and the fish flakes easily with a fork. Divide the fish and vegetables among the serving bowls, over the noodles, and ladle the broth into each.

4. Refrigerate leftover cooled noodles and soba in separate airtight containers for up to 2 days.

Continued ▶

PREP TIP I keep a clean pair of pliers in my kitchen to remove fish bones. Place your fingertips on either side of the bone so the flesh of the fish doesn't tear. Grasp the tip of the bone with the pliers and gently pull to remove.

Per Serving: Total calories: 414; Total fat: 10g; Saturated fat: 1g; Carbohydrates: 50g; Sodium: 1,259mg; Fiber: 4g; Protein: 32g

KALE AND ORZO MINESTRONE WITH PISTOU

Easy Prep

Serves: 6

Prep time:
15 minutes

Cook time:
45 minutes

This is a springtime take on classic minestrone. It uses kale in two ways, simmered in the broth and blended into the *pistou*, which is just a fancy Provençal name for pesto. Research confirms that cooked kale is as healthy as raw kale, but in a different way. Cooking breaks down the vegetable's cell walls, making some nutrients more bioavailable. Keeping it raw retains kale's antioxidants.

¼ cup plus 2 tablespoons extra-virgin olive oil, divided

6 garlic cloves, minced, divided

1 onion, minced

8 ounces orzo pasta

Sea salt

Freshly ground black pepper

1 bunch kale, stems finely chopped, leaves thinly sliced

4 quarts Roasted Vegetable Broth (page 4)

1 cup fresh or frozen peas

2 cups fresh basil

¼ cup freshly grated Parmesan cheese

Zest of ½ lemon

Juice of ½ lemon

1. In a large pot over medium heat, heat 2 tablespoons of olive oil. Reserve ½ teaspoon of garlic. Add the onion and remaining garlic to the pot and cook for about 5 minutes, until the onion begins to soften.

2. Add the orzo to the pot and cook for 1 to 2 minutes until well coated in the oil. Season with salt and pepper.

3. Reserve 1 cup of the kale leaves for the pistou. Add the remaining kale leaves and stems and vegetable broth to the pot and bring the soup to a simmer. Cook for about 10 minutes, or until the kale and orzo are tender.

4. Stir in the peas.

Continued ▶

5. While the soup cooks, make the pistou. In a blender, combine the remaining ¼ cup of olive oil, reserved ½ teaspoon of garlic, reserved 1 cup of kale leaves, and the basil. Pulse a few times until the leaves are broken down. Stir in the Parmesan cheese and lemon zest. Season with salt, pepper, and lemon juice.

6. Serve the soup immediately topped with the pistou, or cover and refrigerate for up 3 days.

SUBSTITUTE IT! If you'd like to try another grain for this soup, use *freekeh*, which is wheat grains that have been roasted and rubbed to give them a toasty flavor and nutty texture. Freekeh is a good source of fiber, which helps prevent all cancers, stroke, diabetes, and heart disease. I use whole-grain freekeh and increase the cook time in step 3 to 25 minutes; if you can only find the cracked variety, use a cook time of 20 minutes, or cook until the grains are tender.

Per Serving: Total calories: 547; Total fat: 27g; Saturated fat: 3g; Carbohydrates: 64g; Sodium: 212mg; Fiber: 9g; Protein: 17g

SWEET MISO AND CARROT NOODLE SOUP

Dairy-Free
Vegan
Serves: 4
Prep time: 15 minutes
Cook time: 10 minutes

The broth in this soup is downright addicting! But unlike other foods that tempt you to eat more than you care to, this is actually good for you. The miso offers plenty of probiotics, and carrot noodles lend a vibrant, healthy note to traditional rice noodles. Cabbage and other cruciferous vegetables here are potent cancer fighters.

4 ounces thin rice noodles

2 carrots, peeled

1 tablespoon toasted sesame oil, plus more for serving

1 tablespoon minced peeled fresh ginger

1 teaspoon minced garlic

2 tablespoons soy sauce (gluten-free, if needed), plus more for serving

2 tablespoons rice wine vinegar

2 tablespoons maple syrup or light brown sugar

2 quarts Miso Broth (page 9)

4 cups shredded Napa cabbage

1. Put the rice noodles in a heatproof bowl and cover them with hot water. Set aside for 10 minutes to soften.

2. Trim the stem end from the carrots and halve them widthwise so you have two roughly 4-inch segments. One at a time, fit them onto a spiralizer and run through the smallest noodle setting. Set aside.

3. In a large pot over medium heat, heat the sesame oil. Add the ginger and garlic. Cook for about 1 minute, until fragrant. Whisk in the soy sauce, vinegar, and maple syrup.

4. Add the miso broth and bring the soup to a gentle simmer.

5. Add the cabbage and cook for 2 minutes.

6. Stir in the carrot noodles and cook for 2 minutes more.

Continued ▶

7. Drain the rice noodles and stir them into the soup. Divide the soup among serving bowls and serve with additional soy sauce and toasted sesame oil on the side.

SUBSTITUTE IT! If you can't find Napa cabbage, regular green cabbage or bok choy works just fine.

Per Serving: Total calories: 256; Total fat: 4g; Saturated fat: 1g; Carbohydrates: 50g; Sodium: 1,203mg; Fiber: 4g; Protein: 6g

VEGETABLE PHO

Dairy-Free
Gluten-Free
Vegan
Serves: 4
Prep time:
20 minutes
Cook time:
40 minutes

Traditional pho is all about the meat, broth, and garnishes. This plant-based version attempts to keep the original characteristics of the soup while boosting its nutritional value. Seared portobello mushrooms replace meat, brown rice noodles stand in for refined white rice noodles, and it includes a handful of fresh vegetables.

8 ounces wide brown rice noodles

1 yellow onion, halved

2 whole cloves

1 whole cinnamon stick

1 star anise

2-inch piece fresh ginger, halved

1½ quarts Superfood Vegetable Broth (page 2)

2 tablespoons gluten-free soy sauce

2 tablespoons canola oil

2 portobello mushrooms, cut into slices

Sea salt

1 cup snow peas, halved

1 carrot, julienned

1 cup mung bean sprouts

Large handful fresh herbs, such as mint, cilantro, and Thai basil

1 lime, cut into wedges

1. Bring a medium pot of salted water to a boil over high heat. Add the brown rice noodles. Remove the pan from the heat and let the noodles soak for 10 minutes, or until completely soft. Drain and set aside.

2. Heat a large pot over medium-high heat. When hot, add the onion, cut-side down. Cook for 4 to 5 minutes without moving. Flip the onion over and add the cloves, cinnamon stick, and star anise to the pot. Toast the spices for about 1 minute until fragrant.

Continued ▶

3. Carefully add the ginger and vegetable broth and bring the soup to a simmer. Reduce the heat to low and cook at a gentle simmer for 15 minutes. Strain the broth through a fine-mesh sieve set over another pot to remove the solids. Discard the solids. Return the broth to the pot and keep warm. Stir in soy sauce.

4. Heat a large sauté pan or skillet over medium-high heat. When hot, pour in the canola oil and tilt the skillet to coat the bottom. Sear the mushroom slices for 3 to 4 minutes on each side, until browned. Season with salt.

5. Divide the noodles among serving dishes. Add the snow peas and carrot. Divide the broth among the bowls. Top with the seared mushrooms, bean sprouts, fresh herbs, and a lime wedge.

6. Refrigerate leftover noodles and broth separately in airtight containers for up to 3 days.

PREP TIP Have all the ingredients measured and prepped before you begin cooking to make this soup as easy as possible to come together.

Per Serving: Total calories: 334; Total fat: 9g; Saturated fat: 1g; Carbohydrates: 59g; Sodium: 723mg; Fiber: 9g; Protein: 9g

LENTIL PENNE
TOMATO BASIL SOUP

Dairy-Free
Easy Prep
Gluten-Free
Vegan
Serves: 4
Prep time:
5 minutes
Cook time:
35 minutes

Pasta made with red lentil flour is my new favorite. It has more than 10 grams of protein per serving, so if I'm making a plant-based meal, I don't have to think of a separate protein source to add. It also has a lot more fiber than traditional whole-wheat pasta. As it cooks, the lentil pasta releases starch, which thickens the soup beautifully.

2 tablespoons
  extra-virgin
  olive oil

1 small onion, minced

4 garlic cloves, minced

Pinch red
  pepper flakes

1 (28-ounce) can
  plum tomatoes,
  hand crushed

2 cups roughly
  chopped fresh
  basil, divided

¼ cup dry white wine

2 quarts Roasted
  Vegetable Broth
  (page 4), or
  Superfood Vegetable
  Broth (page 2)

8 ounces lentil
  penne pasta

Sea salt

Freshly ground
  black pepper

1. In a large pot over medium-high heat, heat the olive oil. Add the onion, garlic, and red pepper flakes. Cook for about 10 minutes, until the onion is soft, being careful not to burn the garlic.

2. Add the tomatoes and 1 cup of basil. Cook for about 10 minutes until very fragrant and much of the liquid has evaporated. Add the white wine to the pot and cook for 2 minutes more.

3. Add the vegetable broth and bring the soup to a simmer.

Continued ▶

4. Add the pasta to the pot, season with salt and pepper, and cook for 10 minutes, or until the pasta is tender. Stir in the remaining 1 cup of basil.

5. Refrigerate cooled leftovers in an airtight container for up to 3 days.

TASTE TIP If you can eat dairy, the soup is delicious topped with plenty of freshly grated Parmesan cheese.

Per Serving: Total calories: 318; Total fat: 9g; Saturated fat: 1g; Carbohydrates: 49g; Sodium: 545mg; Fiber: 11g; Protein: 17g

GINGER CORN RICE NOODLE SOUP

Dairy-Free
Easy Prep
Gluten-Free
Serves: 4
Prep time:
5 minutes
Cook time:
15 minutes

Festive and light, this soup is perfect for New Year's. Allow the benefits of ginger—a potent anti-inflammatory with anti-cancer properties—to jump-start your resolutions to eat healthier.

1 tablespoon canola oil

1½ tablespoons minced peeled fresh ginger

1 small garlic clove, minced

1 shallot, minced

¼ teaspoon red pepper flakes

2 quarts Chicken Broth (page 11)

4 ounces thin rice noodles

4 cups frozen corn kernels

2 cups shredded cooked chicken meat

Sea salt

Freshly ground black pepper

Fresh cilantro, for serving

1. In a large pot over medium heat, heat the canola oil. Add the ginger, garlic, shallot, and red pepper flakes. Cook for about 5 minutes, until fragrant and soft, being careful not to burn the garlic.

2. Add the chicken broth and bring the soup to a simmer. Cook for 5 minutes.

3. Stir in the rice noodles and simmer for 3 to 4 minutes, until the noodles are just al dente.

4. Stir in the corn and chicken and simmer for 1 minute more, or until heated through. Taste and season with salt and pepper. Garnish with fresh cilantro.

5. Refrigerate cooled leftovers in an airtight container for up to 2 days.

TASTE TIP You'll need roughly 6 large ears of corn to yield 4 cups kernels.

Per Serving: Total calories: 479; Total fat: 12g; Saturated fat: 2g; Carbohydrates: 67g; Sodium: 369mg; Fiber: 8g; Protein: 30g

Garlic Rosemary
Braised Lamb
and Beans, page 136

CHAPTER SIX

Stews and Chilis

What distinguishes a stew or chili from mere soup? The Internet provides little consensus. Maybe it's viscosity—with a stew, you might be able to stand a spoon in it. Not so with soup. Maybe it's meat—a stew often contains large chunks of meat and vegetables cooked together in a scant amount of liquid, less than soup. Maybe it's the nature of the meal—a stew might feel more like a hearty dinner than soup does. As for chili, the line is even blurrier. Beans or no beans? Tomatoes, yes or no? Is white chili even chili at all?

To be honest, I have no strong opinion on the topic. The recipes in this chapter provide hearty, warming dinners, whatever you call them. They're filled with flavorful vegetables, tender roots, whole grains, legumes, and meat.

SMOKY BLACK-EYED PEA STEW

Dairy-Free
Easy Prep
Gluten-Free
Vegan
Serves: 4
Prep time:
15 minutes
Cook time:
30 minutes

Considered the "holy trinity" of Cajun cooking, onion, bell pepper, and celery form a flavor base in this hearty stew. Black-eyed peas have a distinct, earthy flavor and, like all legumes, they're an excellent source of dietary fiber for a healthy gut biome. Instead of using pork in this stew—a classic ingredient with stewed collard greens and beans in Southern cooking—I use liquid smoke. It gives the stew a delicious complexity without the meat.

2 tablespoons extra-virgin olive oil

1 onion, diced

1 green bell pepper, diced

2 celery stalks, minced

4 garlic cloves, minced

1 tablespoon minced fresh thyme leaves

2 teaspoons Cajun blackening spice

1 (15-ounce) can fire-roasted diced tomatoes

2 (15-ounce) cans black-eyed peas, drained

1 bunch collard greens, thinly sliced

1 quart Roasted Vegetable Broth (page 4)

¼ teaspoon liquid smoke

Sea salt

Freshly ground black pepper

1. In a large pot over medium-high heat, heat the olive oil. Add the onion, bell pepper, and celery. Cook for about 8 minutes, until nearly soft. Add the garlic and cook for 2 minutes more.

2. Add the thyme and blackening spice to the pot and cook for 1 minute, until fragrant.

3. Stir in the tomatoes, black-eyed peas, collard greens, vegetable broth, and ¼ teaspoon liquid smoke. Generously season with salt and pepper. Cover the pot and simmer for 10 to 15 minutes, until the collard greens are soft.

SIMPLIFY IT! If you want to use dried black-eyed peas, soak them in water overnight, then drain. Increase the broth by 1 quart. Add the tomatoes and collard greens to the stew once the black-eyed peas have fully softened. The acid in the tomatoes will interfere with the beans cooking properly.

Per Serving: Total calories: 336; Total fat: 9g; Saturated fat: 1g; Carbohydrates: 50g; Sodium: 350mg; Fiber: 14g; Protein: 16g

MUSHROOM BOURGUIGNON

Dairy-Free
Easy Prep
Gluten-Free
Vegan
Serves: 4
Prep time:
15 minutes
Cook time:
1 hour

When I lived in Europe, one of my favorite French meals to cook was beef bourguignon. It saw me through many dark, rainy winter days. However, my husband is a vegetarian, so I wanted to create a stew with similar flavors without the meat. Mushrooms were the perfect solution. A one-year trial conducted by researchers at Johns Hopkins found that simply swapping mushrooms for red meat resulted in 7 pounds of weight loss, without any other intervention, during that period. This stew is delicious over mashed potatoes or egg noodles.

**2 tablespoons
canola oil**

**4 portobello
mushrooms,
cut into
½-inch-thick slices**

2 carrots, sliced

**1 garlic
clove, smashed**

**2 tablespoons
tomato paste**

**1 tablespoon minced
fresh thyme leaves**

1 cup dry red wine

**1 pound pearl onions
(frozen is fine)**

**1 quart Roasted
Vegetable Broth
(page 4)**

Sea salt

**Freshly ground
black pepper**

1 cup green peas

1. Preheat the oven to 375°F.

2. In a large Dutch oven over medium-high heat, heat the canola oil. Working in batches, sear the mushrooms for 2 to 3 minutes per side, being careful not to crowd the pan, until deeply golden brown. Remove and set aside. Repeat until all the mushrooms have been seared. Return all the mushrooms to the pot, along with any accumulated juices.

3. Add the carrots, garlic, tomato paste, and thyme. Cook for 1 minute.

4. Using a wooden spoon, stir in the red wine, scraping up any browned bits from the bottom of the pan.

5. Add the onions and broth and generously season with salt and pepper. Cover the pan and transfer it to the oven. Cook for 45 minutes.

6. Remove from the oven, and stir in the peas before serving.

7. Refrigerate leftovers in an airtight container for up to 3 days.

POWER UP! Stir in 2 tablespoons of red miso paste just before serving for a boost of umami flavor and healthy probiotics.

Per Serving: Total calories: 313; Total fat: 9g; Saturated fat: 1g; Carbohydrates: 32g; Sodium: 152mg; Fiber: 7g; Protein: 7g

CHICKEN MOLE

Dairy-Free
Gluten-Free
Serves: 4
Prep time:
20 minutes
Cook time:
1 hour, 45 minutes

You might think of mole as meat simmered in a spicy sauce with a hint of chocolate. Technically, that's true. But it's also filled with antioxidant-rich spices, seeds, and vegetables all blended into a velvety sauce. A review published in the journal *Food Science & Nutrition* found that incorporating chiles into your diet has the potential to shore up micronutrient deficiencies. They're also good sources of phytochemicals and dietary fiber. Step aside, multivitamins! To make this dish plant-based, use 4 cups of cooked chickpeas and Superfood Vegetable Broth (page 2) in place of the chicken and chicken broth.

4 dried guajillo chiles

2 dried poblano peppers

2 dried Morita chiles

1 corn tortilla, cut into thin strips

½ cup pepitas

1 teaspoon ground cinnamon

¼ teaspoon ground cloves

1 onion, halved, roots cut away

2 plum tomatoes, halved

½ cup pitted prunes

½ cup diced plantain

4 garlic cloves, smashed

4 ounces Mexican chocolate

4 ounces piloncillo, or light brown sugar

2 quarts Chicken Broth (page 11)

2 teaspoons sea salt, divided

4 cups shredded cooked chicken (from the Chicken Broth recipe)

1. In a medium pot over high heat, bring 2 cups of water to a boil. Add the guajillo, poblano, and Morita chiles to the pot. Cover the pot and simmer for 15 minutes. Remove from the heat and let the chiles soften in the water for 15 minutes more.

2. Heat a large cast-iron skillet over medium-high heat. Working in batches so as not to crowd the pan, individually toast these ingredients: Toast the tortilla strips for 1 to 2 minutes, until browned (but not

burned). Transfer them to a blender. Return the dry skillet to the heat and toast the pepitas, cinnamon, and cloves for about 1 minute, until fragrant. Transfer to the blender. Add the onion halves to the skillet and toast for 3 to 4 minutes, until charred, but not burned; transfer to the blender. Finally, toast the tomatoes in the skillet for 2 to 3 minutes, until browned and fragrant. Add them to the blender.

3. Add the prunes, plantain, garlic, and steamed chiles to the blender, along with enough of the chile cooking liquid to initiate movement. Blend until smooth. Return the mixture to the skillet, place the skillet over medium heat, and bring the mixture to a gentle simmer.

4. Stir in the chocolate, piloncillo, chicken broth, and 1 teaspoon of salt. Simmer, uncovered, for 1 hour, until thick and fragrant, stirring occasionally to keep it from sticking. It will continue to thicken and intensify in flavor as it cooks.

5. During the last 15 minutes of cook time, stir in the chicken.

6. Taste and season with the remaining salt, as needed.

7. Refrigerate leftovers in an airtight container for up to 4 days.

PREP TIP To avoid the acrid taste present in some moles, avoid blackening the onion and other ingredients toasted in step 2.

Per Serving: Total calories: 735; Total fat: 25g; Saturated fat: 7g; Carbohydrates: 82g; Sodium: 1,629mg; Fiber: 9g; Protein: 51g

FIRE-ROASTED VEGAN CHILI

Dairy-Free
Gluten-Free
Vegan
Serves: 4
Prep time:
15 minutes
Cook time:
45 minutes

When you're making vegan chili, every ingredient has to bring flavor, texture, and nutrition to the dish. There's no coasting along on the coattails of ground beef. In this vegan chili, tender onions, carrots, and celery infuse it with flavor. Traditional spices include cumin, smoked paprika, and chili powder. For a burst of umami, I sear mushrooms until well browned. Fire-roasted tomatoes offer even more umami and a nice bit of smokiness.

4 tablespoons canola oil, divided

1 onion, diced

1 carrot, diced

1 celery stalk, diced

Sea salt

2 cups sliced button mushrooms

2 bell peppers, assorted colors, cored and sliced

4 garlic cloves, minced

1 tablespoon ground cumin

1 tablespoon smoked paprika

1 tablespoon chili powder

¼ teaspoon ground cinnamon

2 (15-ounce) cans fire-roasted diced tomatoes

2 (15-ounce) cans chili beans

Freshly ground black pepper

1. In a large pot over medium heat, heat 2 tablespoons of the canola oil. Add the onion, carrot, celery, and a pinch of salt. Cook for about 10 minutes, until the vegetables are very soft.

2. While the vegetables cook, in a large sauté pan or skillet over medium-high heat, heat the remaining 2 tablespoons of canola oil. Add the mushrooms and sear for about 3 minutes per side, or until they're golden brown. Add the cooked mushrooms to the pot along with the bell peppers and garlic. Cook for 2 minutes.

3. Stir in the cumin, paprika, chili powder, and cinnamon. Cook for 1 minute to toast the spices.

4. Stir in the tomatoes and chili beans. Simmer the chili, uncovered, for 30 minutes to allow all the flavors to come together. Taste and season with salt and pepper.

5. Refrigerate leftovers in an airtight container for up to 3 days.

PREP TIP Save all the vegetable scraps from this recipe and you'll have everything you need to make a batch of the Superfood Vegetable Broth (page 2).

Per Serving: Total calories: 381; Total fat: 17g; Saturated fat: 2g; Carbohydrates: 52g; Sodium: 1,300mg; Fiber: 15g; Protein: 14g

SWEET POTATO, APPLE, AND CABBAGE STEW WITH CHICKEN SAUSAGE

Dairy-Free
Easy Prep
Gluten-Free
Serves: 4
Prep time:
15 minutes

Cook time:
35 minutes, plus
10 minutes to rest

This comforting fall stew is built around three superfoods—sweet potato, apple, and cabbage. Cabbage is the clear leader of the pack. In a study titled "Food as Pharma? The Case of Glucosinolates," researchers identified brassicas, including cabbage, as protective and possibly even therapeutic against cancer.

2 tablespoons extra-virgin olive oil

1 small red onion, halved and cut into slices

1 pound chicken sausage links

2 large sweet potatoes, peeled and cut into 2-inch pieces

2 Granny Smith apples, peeled, cored, and cut into wedges

½ head green cabbage, cut into 1-inch-wide strips

1 quart Chicken Broth (page 11)

4 thyme sprigs

1 whole cinnamon stick (optional)

Sea salt

1. Preheat the oven to 400°F.

2. Heat a large Dutch oven over medium-high heat. Pour in the olive oil and red onion and sauté for 3 minutes, until the onion begins to soften.

3. Add the chicken sausages and cook for about 2 minutes per side, until beginning to brown, but not cooked through.

4. Add the sweet potatoes, apples, cabbage, chicken broth, thyme, and cinnamon stick. Season with salt. Cover the pan and transfer it to the oven. Cook for 25 minutes, until the vegetables are tender and the sausages are cooked through. Let rest for 10 minutes before serving.

5. Refrigerate leftovers in an airtight container for up to 2 days.

SIMPLIFY IT! The whole dish can be made in a slow cooker. Omit the oil and add all the other ingredients to the slow cooker. Cover the cooker and cook on low heat for 6 to 8 hours, or until the vegetables are tender and the sausages are cooked through.

Per Serving: Total calories: 450; Total fat: 17g; Saturated fat: 4g; Carbohydrates: 53g; Sodium: 801mg; Fiber: 9g; Protein: 24g

CHICKEN CHILI VERDE
WITH TOMATILLO SALSA

Dairy-Free Option

Gluten-Free Option

Serves: 4

Prep time: 20 minutes

Cook time: 30 minutes

The first time you use tomatillos, after discarding the husk, you may be surprised by their sticky coating. That sticky material has anti-inflammatory properties equivalent to over-the-counter drugs like ibuprofen.

For the stew

1 yellow onion, quartered

2 poblano peppers, halved lengthwise and cored

2 jalapeño peppers, halved lengthwise and cored

8 medium tomatillos, husked and halved

8 garlic cloves, unpeeled

2 tablespoons canola oil

Sea salt

Freshly ground black pepper

1 tablespoon ground cumin

1 tablespoon freshly squeezed lime juice

1 (15-ounce) can chickpeas, drained

1 quart Chicken Broth (page 11)

4 cups shredded cooked chicken (from the Chicken Broth recipe)

Sour cream, for serving (optional)

Blue corn tortilla chips (for serving)

For the salsa

4 medium tomatillos, husked and finely diced

1 jalapeño pepper, minced

½ small red onion, minced

1 garlic clove, minced

½ cup minced fresh cilantro

2 tablespoons freshly squeezed lime juice

Sea salt

To make the stew

1. Preheat the oven to 400°F.

2. Spread the onion, poblanos, jalapeños, tomatillos, and garlic in a single layer on a rimmed sheet pan. Drizzle with the canola oil and gently toss to coat. Season with salt and pepper.

3. Roast for 20 minutes, or until the fruit and vegetables are tender and beginning to brown. Let cool.

4. When the mixture is cool enough to handle, peel the garlic cloves. Transfer the contents to a blender and blend until mostly smooth. Set aside.

5. Heat a large pot over medium heat. Add the cumin and toast for 1 minute, until fragrant.

6. Add the tomatillo puree, lime juice, chickpeas, chicken broth, and chicken. Cook for 10 minutes. Taste and season with salt and pepper.

To make the salsa

1. In a small bowl, stir together the tomatillos, jalapeño, red onion, garlic, cilantro, and lime juice until combined. Season with salt.

2. Top each bowl of stew with a generous spoonful of salsa, a dollop of sour cream (if using), and a handful of chips (if using). Cover and refrigerate leftovers in separate airtight containers for up to 2 days.

SIMPLIFY IT! To make the stew in a slow cooker with raw chicken, prepare the tomatillo puree through step 4 (to make the stew). Add it to a slow cooker along with the cumin, lime juice, chicken broth, and 1 pound of raw chicken tenders or sliced chicken breast. Cover the cooker and cook on low heat for 6 hours. Stir in the chickpeas. Taste and season with salt and pepper. Make the salsa as directed and serve with the stew.

Per Serving: Total calories: 536; Total fat: 21g; Saturated fat: 4g; Carbohydrates: 37g; Sodium: 256mg; Fiber: 11g; Protein: 48g

RED BEAN CHILI WITH
ROASTED PEPPERS AND MILLET

Dairy-Free
Gluten-Free
Vegan
Serves: 4
Prep time:
10 minutes
Cook time:
35 minutes

Millet provides texture and body to this hearty vegetarian chili. Together, millet and kidney beans are good sources of phytates, which help detoxify heavy metals. Cilantro has similar properties and serves as a refreshing garnish to this dish.

**2 tablespoons
   extra-virgin
   olive oil**

1 yellow onion, diced

**4 garlic
   cloves, minced**

**1 tablespoon
   chili powder**

**1 tablespoon
   smoked paprika**

**1 teaspoon
   ground cumin**

**1 quart Superfood
   Vegetable Broth
   (page 2)**

**1 (15-ounce) can
   fire-roasted
   tomatoes**

**1 (12-ounce) jar
   roasted red
   peppers, drained
   and sliced**

½ cup millet

**2 (15-ounce) cans
   kidney beans,
   rinsed and drained**

**1 tablespoon freshly
   squeezed lime juice**

Sea salt

**½ cup minced
   fresh cilantro**

1. In a large pot over medium heat, heat the olive oil. Add the onion and garlic. Cook for 8 to 10 minutes until soft, being careful not to burn the garlic.

2. Stir in the chili powder, paprika, and cumin. Cook for about 1 minute, until the spices are fragrant.

3. Add the vegetable broth, tomatoes, red peppers, and millet. Bring the chili to a simmer. Cover the pot and cook for 15 minutes, or until the millet is soft.

4. Stir in the kidney beans and lime juice. Taste and season with salt. Cook for 2 to 3 minutes.

5. Divide the soup among serving dishes and top with the cilantro. Or, cover and refrigerate for up to 3 days.

SIMPLIFY IT! This chili can also be made in a slow cooker. Put all the ingredients into the slow cooker, cover the cooker, and cook on low heat for 6 hours, or until the millet is soft.

Per Serving: Total calories: 373; Total fat: 2g; Saturated fat: 0g; Carbohydrates: 70g; Sodium: 624mg; Fiber: 16g; Protein: 19g

GARLIC ROSEMARY BRAISED LAMB AND BEANS

Dairy-Free
Easy Prep
Gluten-Free
Serves: 4
Prep time:
10 minutes
Cook time:
1 hour, 30 minutes, plus
15 minutes for resting

This hearty stew includes pungent rosemary and garlic, tender braised lamb, and soft white beans. I eat red meat infrequently, but when I do, I choose grass-fed beef and lamb. Not only is it the natural diet of ruminants, such as cows and lamb, but also the fatty acid composition yields a higher ratio of omega-3 fats to omega-6 fats. Omega-3 fatty acids are thought to exhibit an anti-inflammatory effect. Browning the meat first is a typical preparation for stews, but it yields advanced glycation end-products. Braising in liquid is a healthier method for preparing meat.

2 tablespoons
 extra-virgin
 olive oil

2 shallots,
 thinly sliced

1½ pounds lamb
 shoulder, cut into
 2-inch pieces

2 tablespoons
 minced fresh
 rosemary leaves

Sea salt

Freshly ground
 black pepper

½ cup dry red wine

2 cups Chicken
 Broth (page 11)

4 garlic
 cloves, smashed

1 (15-ounce) can
 Great Northern or
 cannellini beans

1. Preheat the oven to 350°F.

2. In a large Dutch oven over medium-high heat, heat the olive oil. Add the shallot and cook for 2 minutes.

3. Pat the lamb dry with paper towels and generously season it with the rosemary, salt, and pepper. Add it to the pan along with the red wine, chicken broth, and garlic. Bring the mixture to a simmer. Cover the pan and transfer it to the oven. Cook for 1 ½ hours, or until the lamb is very tender.

4. Stir in the beans. Let the stew rest for 15 minutes before serving.

5. Refrigerate leftovers in an airtight container for up to 2 days.

TASTE TIP If you prefer beef, use chuck roast in place of the lamb.

Per Serving: Total calories: 440; Total fat: 18g; Saturated fat: 5g; Carbohydrates: 22g; Sodium: 223mg; Fiber: 5g; Protein: 41g

BISON BARLEY STEW

Dairy-Free
Easy Prep
Serves: 4
Prep time:
10 minutes
Cook time:
1 hour, 40 minutes

Bison is growing in popularity and for good reason. It's a more environmentally sustainable meat than beef. And according to a double-blind trial published in the journal *Nutrition Research*, it may even be healthier than beef. Compared to beef, bison resulted in less C-reactive protein, a marker of inflammation.

2 tablespoons
   extra-virgin
   olive oil

1 onion, diced

1½ pounds bison
   roast, cut into
   2-inch chunks

Sea salt

Freshly ground
   black pepper

4 garlic
   cloves, minced

2 carrots, sliced

2 cups sliced
   button mushrooms

1 cup dry red wine

1½ quarts Chicken
   Broth (page 11) or
   Roasted Vegetable
   Broth (page 4)

3 tablespoons
   tomato paste

1 teaspoon
   Dijon mustard

1 tablespoon minced
   fresh thyme leaves

1 cup dried barley

1. In a large pot over medium-high heat, heat the olive oil. Add the onion and cook for 5 minutes, until it begins to soften.

2. Season the bison with salt and pepper and add to the pot along with the garlic, carrots, mushrooms, red wine, chicken broth, tomato paste, mustard, and thyme. Bring the stew to a simmer.

3. Add the barley and partially cover the pot. Cook for 1½ hours, or until the bison is tender.

SUBSTITUTE IT! To make this gluten-free, use wild rice. Add it during the last 45 minutes of cooking.

Per Serving: Total calories: 576; Total fat: 14g; Saturated fat: 3g; Carbohydrates: 54g; Sodium: 504mg; Fiber: 12g; Protein: 48g

ROOT VEGETABLE CASSOULET

Dairy-Free
Gluten-Free
Serves: 4
Prep time:
15 minutes
Cook time:
1 hour

Traditional cassoulet is a warming stew of beans and several types of meat simmered for hours in duck fat—not exactly health food. This version keeps the spirit of the original dish while cutting back on the meat and animal fat in favor of tender root vegetables. Umami-rich mushroom broth makes the dish taste as luxurious as the original and is a healthier, superfood option.

¼ cup extra-virgin olive oil

1 cup minced onion

½ cup minced celery

½ cup minced carrot

Sea salt

½ cup dry white wine

2 garlic cloves, minced

1 tablespoon fresh thyme leaves

⅛ teaspoon ground nutmeg

2 cups diced butternut squash

2 (15-ounce) cans cannellini beans, rinsed and drained

1 rutabaga, peeled and diced

1 quart Mushroom Broth (page 6) or Chicken Broth (page 11)

1 pound skinless chicken drumsticks

Freshly ground black pepper

1. In a large pot over medium heat, heat the olive oil. Add the onion, celery, carrot, and a generous pinch of salt. Cook for 15 minutes, until the vegetables are very tender.

2. Stir in the white wine, garlic, thyme, and nutmeg. Cook for 2 minutes to evaporate most of the alcohol.

3. Add the squash, beans, rutabaga, and mushroom broth. Bring the mixture to a simmer.

Continued ▶

4. Nestle the chicken among the vegetables. Season with salt and pepper. Cover the pot and cook for 30 to 40 minutes, until the chicken is cooked through and the vegetables are tender.

5. Refrigerate leftovers in an airtight container for up to 3 days.

TASTE TIP For a more authentic taste, cook 4 ounces diced pancetta in the pot for 5 minutes before proceeding with step 1.

Per Serving: Total calories: 587; Total fat: 20g; Saturated fat: 3g; Carbohydrates: 63g; Sodium: 151mg; Fiber: 17g; Protein: 37g

CHICKPEA MASALA

Dairy-Free
Easy Prep
Gluten-Free
Vegan
Serves: 4
Prep time:
20 minutes
Cook time:
25 minutes

Blended into creamy hummus or roasted to crispy perfection, chickpeas are a versatile superfood. They boast the same benefits as other legumes—loads of fiber, phytates, and potassium—and they have a nice chewy texture that's a good replacement for meat. In this classic Indian stew, they soak up all the delicious spices in the broth—cinnamon, ginger, cardamom, and garam masala. Like most stews, this is delicious served over rice. For an authentic meal, serve with pillowy naan.

1 teaspoon
ground cumin

1 teaspoon
ground coriander

1 tablespoon
coconut oil

1½ cups minced red
onion, divided

1 tablespoon minced
peeled fresh ginger

1 serrano
chile, minced

½ cup tomato puree
(see tip)

½ teaspoon
ground turmeric

½ teaspoon
garam masala

Pinch
ground cinnamon

⅛ teaspoon ground
cardamom, or three
cardamom pods

1 bay leaf

2 (15-ounce) cans
chickpeas, drained
but not rinsed

2 cups Superfood
Vegetable Broth
(page 2)

Sea salt

Freshly ground
black pepper

½ cup roughly
chopped
fresh cilantro

2 tablespoons
freshly squeezed
lemon juice

Steamed basmati
rice, for serving

1. Heat a large pot over medium heat. Add the cumin and coriander and toast for about 1 minute, until fragrant. Add the coconut oil to melt.

2. Add 1 cup of red onion, the ginger, and serrano. Cook for about 5 minutes, or until soft.

Continued ▶

3. Stir in the tomato puree, turmeric, garam masala, cinnamon, cardamom, bay leaf, chickpeas, and vegetable broth. Season with salt and pepper. Bring the stew to a simmer and cook, uncovered, for 20 minutes, until thick and fragrant.

4. In a small bowl, stir together the remaining ½ cup of red onion, the cilantro, lemon juice, and a generous pinch of salt.

5. Divide the stew among serving dishes alongside basmati rice and garnish with the onion-cilantro mixture.

6. Refrigerate leftovers in separate airtight containers; the rice and stew will keep for up to 3 days; the garnish will keep for 1 day.

PREP TIP To make the tomato puree, blend canned diced tomatoes until smooth.

Per Serving: Total calories: 289; Total fat: 6g; Saturated fat: 3g; Carbohydrates: 50g; Sodium: 491mg; Fiber: 13g; Protein: 13g

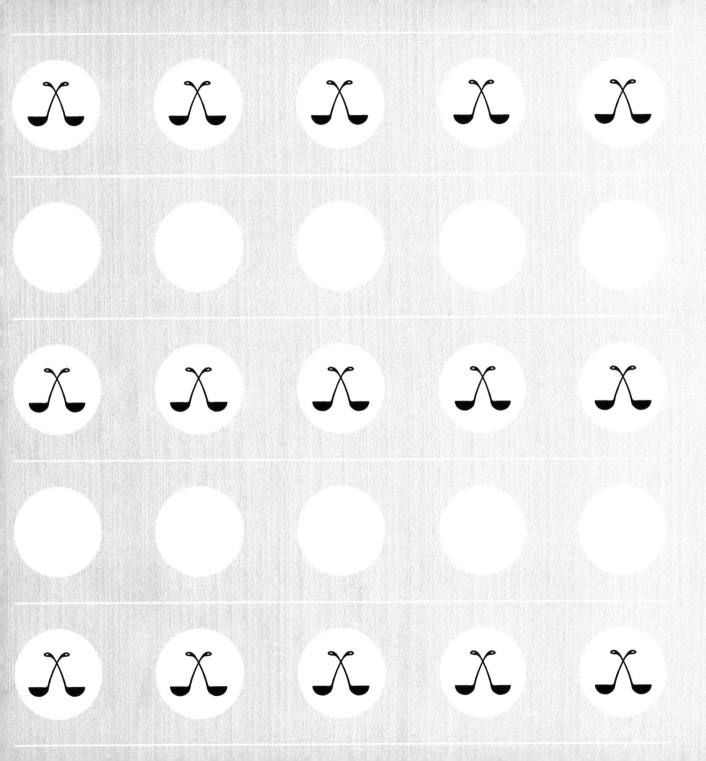

CONVERSION CHART

VOLUME EQUIVALENTS (LIQUID)

US STANDARD	US STANDARD (OUNCES)	METRIC (APPROXIMATE)
2 tablespoons	1 fl. oz.	30 mL
¼ cup	2 fl. oz.	60 mL
½ cup	4 fl. oz.	120 mL
1 cup	8 fl. oz.	240 mL
1½ cups	12 fl. oz.	355 mL
2 cups or 1 pint	16 fl. oz.	475 mL
4 cups or 1 quart	32 fl. oz.	1 L
1 gallon	128 fl. oz.	4 L

VOLUME EQUIVALENTS (DRY)

US STANDARD	METRIC (APPROXIMATE)
⅛ teaspoon	0.5 mL
¼ teaspoon	1 mL
½ teaspoon	2 mL
¾ teaspoon	4 mL
1 teaspoon	5 mL
1 tablespoon	15 mL
¼ cup	59 mL
⅓ cup	79 mL
½ cup	118 mL
⅔ cup	156 mL
¾ cup	177 mL
1 cup	235 mL
2 cups or 1 pint	475 mL
3 cups	700 mL
4 cups or 1 quart	1 L

OVEN TEMPERATURES

FAHRENHEIT (F)	CELSIUS (C) (APPROXIMATE)
250°F	120°C
300°F	150°C
325°F	165°C
350°F	180°C
375°F	190°C
400°F	200°C
425°F	220°C
450°F	230°C

WEIGHT EQUIVALENTS

US STANDARD	METRIC (APPROXIMATE)
½ ounce	15 g
1 ounce	30 g
2 ounces	60 g
4 ounces	115 g
8 ounces	225 g
12 ounces	340 g
16 ounces or 1 pound	455 g

REFERENCES

Akira, I., et al. "Beneficial Effects of a Beta-Cryptoxanthin-Containing Beverage on Body Mass Index and Visceral Fat in Pre-Obese Men: Double-Blind, Placebo-Controlled Parallel Trials." *Journal of Functional Foods* 41 (February 2018): 250–257. doi:/10.1016/j.jff.2017.12.040.

Alali, F. Q., et al. "Garlic for Cardiovascular Disease: Prevention or Treatment?" *Current Pharmaceutical Design* 23, no. 7 (2017): 1028–1041. doi:10.2174/1381612822666161010124530.

Angeloni, C., et al. "Bioactivity of Olive Oil Phenols in Neuroprotection." *International Journal of Molecular Sciences* 18, no. 11 (October 25, 2017): ii. doi:10.3390/ijms18112230.

Bahadoran, Z., et al. "Broccoli Sprouts Reduce Oxidative Stress in Type 2 Diabetes: A Randomized Double-Blind Clinical Trial." *European Journal of Clinical Nutrition* 65, no. 8 (August 2011): 972–7. doi:10.1038/ejcn.2011.59.

Beręsewicz, Andrzej, and Anna Gajos-Draus. "Enjoy Your Heart-Beets. The Role of Dietary Inorganic Nitrate in Cardiovascular Health." *Polish Heart Journal* (2014). doi:/10.5603/KP.a2016.0028.

Bulló, M., et al. "Nutrition Attributes and Health Effects of Pistachio Nuts." *The British Journal of Nutrition*, 115, Supplement 2 (April 2015): S79–93. doi:/10.1017/S0007114514003250.

Capuano, E., et al. "Food as Pharma? The Case of Glucosinolates." *Current Pharmaceutical Design* 23, no. 19 (2017): 2697–2721. doi:/10.2174/1381612823666170120160832.

Cather, Willa. *Death Comes for the Archbishop.* London: Vintage Classics, 1990.

Center for Science in the Public Interest. "10 Best Foods." nutritionaction.com /wp-content/free-downloads/What_To_Eat_com-we-1.pdf. Accessed October 27, 2019.

Centers for Disease Control and Prevention. "Defining Powerhouse Fruits and Vegetables; A Nutrient Density Approach." cdc.gov/pcd/issues/2014/13_0390.htm. Accessed November 26, 2019.

Chen, S., et al. "Anti-Aromatase Activity of Phytochemicals in White Button Mushrooms (Agaricus bisporus)." *Cancer Research* 66, no. 24 (December 15, 2006): 12026–34. doi:10.1158/0008-5472.CAN-06-2206.

Clark, Melissa. *Dinner: Changing the Game*. New York: Clarkson Potter, 2017.

Colwin, Laurie. *Home Cooking: A Writer in the Kitchen*. New York: Vintage. 2010.

Cormio, L., et al. "Oral L-Citrulline Supplementation Improves Erection Hardness in Men with Mild Erectile Dysfunction." *Urology* 77, no. 1 (January 2011): 119–22. doi:10.1016/j.urology.2010.08.028.

Demirel, G., et al. "Fatty Acids of Lamb Meat from Two Breeds Fed Different Forage: Concentrate Ratio." *Meat Science* 72, no. 2 (February 2006): 229–35. doi:10.1016/j.meatsci.2005.07.006.

Fernando, W. M., et al. "The Role of Dietary Coconut for the Prevention and Treatment of Alzheimer's Disease: Potential Mechanisms of Action." *British Journal of Nutrition* 114, no. 1 (July 14, 2015): 1–14. doi:10.1017/S0007114515001452.

Figueroa, A,. et al. "Influence of L-Citrulline and Watermelon Supplementation on Vascular Function and Exercise Performance." *Current Opinion in Clinical Nutrition Metabolic Care* 20, no. 1 (January 2017): 92–98. doi:10.1097/MCO.0000000000000340.

Ganesan, K., et al. "Polyphenol-Rich Lentils and Their Health-Promoting Effects." *International Journal of Molecular Sciences* 18, no. 11 (November 2017): ii. doi:10.3390/ijms18112390.

Giménez-Bastida, J. A., and H. Zieliński. "Buckwheat as a Functional Food and Its Effects on Health." *Journal of Agricultural and Food Chemistry* 63, no. 36 (September 2015): 7896–913. doi:10.1021/acs.jafc.5b02498.

Greger, Michael, MD. *How Not to Die: Discover the Foods Scientifically Proven to Prevent and Reverse Disease*. New York: Flatiron Books, 2015.

Greger, Michael, MD. "Superfood Bargains, Volume 2." (September 22, 2008). NutritionFacts.org. nutritionfacts.org/video/superfood-bargains-2/.

Kalita, S., et al. "Almonds and Cardiovascular Health: A Review." *Nutrients* 10, no. 4 (April 2018): ii. doi:10.3390/nu10040468.

Khadivzadeh, T., et al. "Effect of Fennel on the Health Status of Menopausal Women: A Systematic and Meta-Analysis." *Journal of Menopausal Medicine* 24, no. 1 (April 2018): 67–74. doi:10.6118/jmm.2018.24.1.67.

Li, C., et al. "Serum α-Carotene Concentrations and Risk of Death Among US Adults: The Third National Health and Nutrition Examination Survey Follow-Up Study." *Archives of Internal Medicine* 171, no. 6 (March 28, 2011): 507–15. doi:10.1001/archinternmed.2010.440.

Li, F., et al. "Fish Consumption and Risk of Depression: A Meta-Analysis." *Journal of Epidemiology and Community Health* 70, no. 3 (March 2016): 299–304. doi:10.1136/jech-2015-206278.

Mah, E., et al., "Cashew Consumption Reduces Total and LDL Cholesterol: A Randomized, Crossover, Controlled-Feeding Trial." *American Journal of Clinical Nutrition* 105, no. 5 (May 2017): 1070–1078. doi:10.3945/ajcn.116.150037.

McDaniel, J., et al. "Bison Meat Has a Lower Atherogenic Risk Than Beef in Healthy Men." *Nutrition Research* 33, no. 4 (April 2013): 293–302. doi:10.1016/j.nutres.2013.01.007.

McKay, D. L., et al. "Hibiscus sabdariffa L. Tea (Tisane) Lowers Blood Pressure in Prehypertensive and Mildly Hypertensive Adults." *Journal of Nutrition* 140, no. 2 (February 2010): 298–303. doi:10.3945/jn.109.115097.

Messina, M., et al. "Soy and Health Update: Evaluation of the Clinical and Epidemiologic Literature." *Nutrients* 8, no. 12 (November 24, 2016): ii. doi:10.3390/nu8120754.

MicroNourish.com. "Micronutrients: Nutrient Density Guide." Accessed October 27, 2019. micronutrients.com/wp-content/uploads/2015/07/ANDI-chart.pdf.

Miyai, K., et al, "Suppression of Thyroid Function During Ingestion of Seaweed 'Kombu' (Laminaria Japonoca) in Normal Japanese Adults." *Endocrinology Journal* 55, no. 6 (December 2008): 1103–8. doi:10.1507/endocrj.k08e-125.

Moore, Naoko Takei, and Kyle Connaughton. *Donabe: Classic and Modern Japanese Clay Pot Cooking*, New York: Ten Speed Press, 2015.

Morin, Kate. "25 Greatist Superfoods and Why They're Super." *Greatist.* Last modified January 31, 2012. greatist.com/health/25-greatist-superfoods-and-why-theyre-super#4.

Nosrat, Samin. *Salt, Fat, Acid, Heat.* New York: Simon and Schuster, 2019.

Nyakayiru, J., et al. "Beetroot Juice Supplementation Improves High-Intensity Intermittent Type Exercise Performance in Trained Soccer Players." *Nutrients* 9, no. 3 (March 22, 2017): ii. doi:10.3390/nu9030314.

Olatunji, T. L., and A. J. Afolayan. "The Suitability of Chili Pepper (Capsicum annuum L.) for Alleviating Human Micronutrient Dietary Deficiencies: A Review." *Food Science and Nutrition* 6, no. 8 (October 2018): 2239–2251. doi:10.1002/fsn3.790.

Pandey, A. K., et al. "Impact of Stress on Female Reproductive Health Disorders: Possible Beneficial Effects of Shatavari (Asparagus racemosus)." *Biomedical Pharmacotherapy* 103 (July 2018): 46–49. doi:10.1016/j.biopha.2018.04.003.

Poddar, K. H., et al. "Positive Effect of White Button Mushrooms When Substituted for Meat on Body Weight and Composition Changes During Weight Loss and Weight

Maintenance—A One-Year Randomized Clinical Trial." *The FASEB Journal* 27, no. 854 (2013): 4.

Pollan, Michael. *In Defense of Food: An Eater's Manifesto*. New York: Penguin Books, 2009.

Real Hernandez, L. M., et al. "Bean Peptides Have Higher *In Silico* Binding Affinities Than Ezetimibe for the N-Terminal Domain of Cholesterol Receptor Niemann-Pick C1 Like-1." *Peptides* 90 (April 2017): 83–89. doi:10.1016/j.peptides.2017.02.011.

Riso, P., et al. "Effect of 10-Day Broccoli Consumption on Inflammatory Status of Young Healthy Smokers." *International Journal of Food Sciences and Nutrition* 65, no 1. (February 2014): 106–11. doi:10.3109/09637486.2013.830084.

Roncero-Ramos, I., et al. "Effect of Different Cooking Methods on Nutritional Value and Antioxidant Activity of Cultivated Mushrooms." *International Journal of Food Sciences and Nutrition* 68, no. 3 (May 2017): 287–297. doi:10.1080/09637486.2016.1244662.

Sakkas, H., and C. Papadopoulou. "Antimicrobial Activity of Basil, Oregano, and Thyme Essential Oils." *Journal of Microbiology Biotechnology* 27, no. 3 (March 28, 2017): 429–438. doi:10.4014/jmb.1608.08024.

Schlotz, N., et al. "Are Raw Brassica Vegetables Healthier Than Cooked Ones? A Randomized, Controlled Crossover Intervention Trial on the Health-Promoting Potential of Ethiopian Kale." *Nutrients* 10, no. 11 (November 2, 2018): ii. doi:10.3390/nu10111622.

Sultan, M. T., et al. "Immunity: Plants as Effective Mediators." *Critical Reviews in Food Science and Nutrition* 54, no. 10 (2014): 1298–308. doi:10.1080/10408398.2011.633249.

Surendiran, G., et al. "Nutritional Constituents and Health Benefits of Wild Rice (Zizania spp.)" *Nutritional Reviews* 72, no. 4 (April 2014): 227–36. doi:10.1111/nure.12101.

Tang, Y., and R. Tsao. "Phytochemicals in Quinoa and Amaranth Grains and Their Antioxidant, Anti-Inflammatory, and Potential Health Beneficial Effects: A Review." *Molecular Nutrition and Food Research* 61, no. 7 (July 2017). doi:10.1002/mnfr.201600767.

Teas J., et al. "Could Dietary Seaweed Reverse the Metabolic Syndrome?" *Asia Pacific Journal of Clinical Nutrition* 18, no. 2 (2009): 145–54.

Teas, J., et al. "The Consumption of Seaweed as a Protective Factor in the Etiology of Breast Cancer: Proof of Principle." *Journal of Applied Phycology* 25, no. 3 (June 2013): 771–779. doi:10.1007/s10811-012-9931-0.

The Nutrition Source. "Coconut Oil." Harvard T. H. Chan School of Public Health. Accessed October 21, 2019. hsph.harvard.edu/nutritionsource/food-features/coconut-oil/.

Unlu, N., et al. "Carotenoid Absorption from Salad and Salsa by Humans Is Enhanced by the Addition of Avocado or Avocado Oil." *The Journal of Nutrition* 135, no. 3 (March 2005): 431–436. doi:10.1093/jn/135.3.431.

Vaughn, A. R., et al. "Effects of Turmeric (Curcuma longa) on Skin Health: A Systematic Review of the Clinical Evidence." *Phytotherapy Research* 30, no. 8 (August 2016): 1242–1264. doi:10.1002/ptr.5640.

Yagishita, Y., et al. "Broccoli or Sulforaphane: Is It the Source or Dose That Matters?" *Molecules* 24, no. 19 (October 6, 2019): 3593. doi:10.3390/molecules24193593.

Yang, J., and Y. Y. Xiao. "Grape Phytochemicals and Associated Health Benefits." *Critical Reviews in Food Science and Nutrition* 53, no. 11 (2013): 1202–1225. doi:10.1080/10408398.2012.692408.

Zhang, C. R., et al. "New Anti-Inflammatory Sucrose Esters in the Natural Sticky Coating of Tomatillo (Physalis Philadelphica), an Important Culinary Fruit." *Food Chemistry* 196 (April 2016): 726–732. doi:10.1016/j.foodchem.2015.10.007.

Zheng, J., et al. "Spices for Prevention and Treatment of Cancers." *Nutrients* 12, no. 8 (August 2016): ii. doi:10.3390/nu8080495.

RESOURCES

These are some of the books and websites I go to again and again for inspiration and nutrition science.

Books

Campbell, T. Colin. *The China Study: The Most Comprehensive Study of Nutrition Ever Conducted and the Startling Implications for Your Health*. Dallas, TX: BenBella Books, 2006.

Greger, Michael, MD. *How Not to Die: Discover the Foods Scientifically Proven to Prevent and Reverse Disease*. New York: Flatiron Books, 2015.

Pollan, Michael. *In Defense of Food: An Eater's Manifesto*. New York: Penguin Books, 2009.

Websites

Forks Over Knives: ForksOverKnives.com

Harvard Nutrition Science: HSPH.harvard.edu/nutritionsource

New Scientist: NewScientist.com

Nutrition Facts: NutritionFacts.org

PubMed: PubMed.ncbi.nlm.nih.gov

INDEX

ACKNOWLEDGMENTS

Thank you, as always, to the Callisto team for helping shape the best book possible, especially Joe Cho, Kayla Park, and Mary Cassells.

Thank you to the thousands of researchers who pour their lives into studying the effects of what we eat on our health. Your work has the potential to change lives and deserves far more attention than a fleeting media headline. It should inform our everyday lives. Thank you!

Thank you to my family for their tireless support and willingness to endure long days of recipe testing and food photo shoots. I couldn't do it without you.

ABOUT THE AUTHOR

 **PAMELA ELLGEN** is the author of more than a dozen cookbooks, including the bestselling *5-Ingredient College Cookbook*, *The Gluten-Free Cookbook for Families*, and *The Big Dairy Free Cookbook*. Her work has been featured in *Outside Magazine*, TODAY, *Healthline, Huffington Post, Edible Phoenix, Darling Magazine*, and the *Portland Tribune*. Pamela lives in Oceanside, California, with her husband and two sons.

CPSIA information can be obtained
at www.ICGtesting.com
Printed in the USA
BVHW021828210420
578048BV00009B/61